THE COMMONWEALTH AND INTERNATIONAL LIBRARY

Joint Chairmen of the Honorary Editorial Advisory Board

SIR ROBERT ROBINSON, O.M., F.R.S., London, and DEAN ATHELSTAN SPILHAUS, Minnesota

Publisher ROBERT MAXWELL, M.C., M.P.

Education
and Education Research
Division

APPROACHES
TO
ADULT TEACHING

APPROACHES
TO
ADULT TEACHING

Edited by

NORMAN DEES, B.A.

Director of Extra-mural Studies,
University of Glasgow

PERGAMON PRESS

OXFORD · LONDON · EDINBURGH · NEW YORK
PARIS · FRANKFURT

Pergamon Press Ltd., Headington Hill Hall, Oxford
4 & 5 Fitzroy Square, London W.1

Pergamon Press (Scotland) Ltd., 2 & 3 Teviot Place, Edinburgh 1

Pergamon Press Inc., 122 East 55th Street, New York 22, N.Y.

Gauthier-Villars, 55 Quai des Grands-Augustins, Paris 6

Pergamon Press GmbH, Kaiserstrasse 75, Frankfurt-am-Main

Federal Publications Ltd., Times House, River Valley Rd., Singapore

Samcax Book Services Ltd., Queensway, P.O. Box 2720, Nairobi, Kenya.

First edition 1965

Set in 10 on 12pt. Modern
and printed in Great Britain by
A. Brown & Sons, Ltd., Hull, London and Northampton.

CONTENTS

page

FOREWORD   The Right Hon. LORD GREENHILL,   vii
O.B.E., LL.D., J.P.
*Vice-Chairman, Extra-Mural Education
Committee,
University of Glasgow.*

ACKNOWLEDGEMENT   ix

CHAPTER I
Background and   NORMAN DEES, B.A.   1
Forecast   *Director of Extra-Mural Studies,
University of Glasgow.*

CHAPTER II
Archaeology   J. X. W. P. CORCORAN,   17
M.A., Ph.D., F.S.A.
*Department of Archaeology,
University of Glasgow.*

CHAPTER III
History and   H. J. SMITH, M.A., B.Litt. and   36
Politics   J. G. S. SHEARER, M.A.
*Department of Extra-Mural Education,
University of Glasgow.*

CHAPTER IV
Economics   FARQUHAR GILLANDERS, M.A.   56
*Department of Extra-Mural Education,
University of Glasgow.*

CHAPTER V
An Aspect of   R. A. WILLIAMS, M.A.   70
*International
Relations:*   *Department of Extra-Mural Education,
University of Glasgow.*
Asian Studies

CHAPTER VI
Foreign   C. J. TITMUS, B.A., Ph.D.   82
Languages   *Department of Extra-Mural Education,
University of Glasgow.*

CHAPTER VII
English   SARAH DAVIES, M.A., Ph.D.   99
Language and   *Department of English,*
Literature   *University of Glasgow.*

CHAPTER VIII
Art and   MARTIN BAILLIE, D.A. and   123
Music   T. B. WILSON, M.A., B.Mus., A.R.C.M.
                   Department of Extra-Mural Education,
                   University of Glasgow.

CHAPTER IX
Science   WILLIAM C. HUTCHISON,   143
                   B.Sc., Ph.D., F.R.I.C.
                   Department of Extra-Mural Education,
                   University of Glasgow.

CHAPTER X
Psychology   PHILIP A. D. GARDNER,   167
                   M.A., B.Sc., Ed.B., LL.B.
                   Department of Psychology,
                   University of Glasgow.

SELECT BIBLIOGRAPHY   182

APPENDIX   186

FOREWORD

The Right Hon. Lord Greenhill

UNIVERSITY extra-mural tutors, unlike school teachers, do not undergo a period of training lasting two or three years before practising their skills as tutors. They are specialists in particular disciplines, usually with wide-ranging interests, as citizens, in the social, economic, and political problems of the times.

The fact that they have not specifically studied the principles and practices of education as a necessary means of communication does not imply an indifference to their value. On the contrary, the frequent conferences, formal and informal, which extra-mural tutors attend to discuss problems inherent in the teaching of adults, and the literature and periodicals which devote considerable space and thought to these problems, are indications of the concern to establish reliable techniques appropriate to the teaching of adults.

The reasons for this concern are clear. When as a pupil at school the youngster was moved up from one class to another until, at the leaving age, he went into the workshop or college to learn his trade or profession, he was a member of a homogeneous group. According to such interests and capacities as he possessed, his eyes were directed to the adult target which was to provide him with the means of earning his livelihood. His school education was inevitably didactic in spirit, for, made conscious of his own ignorance, he perforce came to rely upon the superior knowledge of his teachers—at least in school-taught subjects.

To see him later as an adult student in an extra-mural class, is to see a quite different being. The men and women who now confront the tutor are no longer school-education dependents. They are now skilled workers, or members of some university-taught profession. Many will be married, some in the early trials of rearing families. They will have voted as electors, influenced by the newspapers and books they favour, by the discussions at work, in the clubs or pubs or social gatherings they frequent. As individuals they are different from one another socially, temperamentally, vocationally, and intellectually. They are in almost every respect a heterogeneous group of individuals brought together by one common aim: the desire to study a particular subject in a collection of subjects offered by an Extra-Mural Committee.

Faced with so mixed a group of adults, how can the tutor establish a workable system of communication with them? Since the normal two-hour period is usually divided between lecture and discussion and, where relevant, demonstration, how can a tutor establish a rapport with the group without ignoring the individual student? How can the individual student be attended to without neglecting the group? And in the many topics which are highly controversial, how can the tutor "objectively" disguise his own views and prejudices without being suspected of being a "propagandist"?

It is its understanding of the problems with which extra-mural tutors have to contend that makes this book by Mr. Norman Dees and his team of tutors so interesting and so helpful. Their contributions are not opinions based upon attractive abstractions. They are the fruits of experience gained in the course of teaching their adult students. Their problems are seen as part of their work, and as their efforts to discover effective teaching techniques. Their findings are not flawless: the trials and treatments are not uniform: and since it is the variables of human behaviour which are being tackled, it would be over-optimism to assume that a final solution is possible.

Fortunately, adult education is rising to a new crest of demand. Interest is increased by every advance in thought. And an educated nation can be judged only by the quality of its adults. In this lies our hope.

ACKNOWLEDGEMENT

The editor wishes to express his thanks to Mr. David Parsons and Miss Elizabeth Hunter for their help in the reading of manuscript and proof.

CHAPTER I

BACKGROUND AND FORECAST

Norman Dees

1. VARIED ORIGINS AND GROWTH

Adult education teaching today is in many respects a product of its historical origins. This is certainly true in some important aspects of the extra-mural teaching of the universities; and it is with this work that this book is chiefly concerned.

It is possible to claim in the most general fashion that the origins of adult education in Great Britain lie in the early Middle Ages.[1] At the same time there is no doubt that, in terms of its present features, the immediately relevant antecedents are no earlier than the eighteenth century. Indeed, for the most part, the nineteenth century is early enough to identify those characteristics which still are to be seen in the attitudes and expectations of the present.

The churches have played an active part in giving to the individual adult a sense of duty in the need to be educated enough to understand the elements of his religious faith. Nonconformists in particular, with their great stress on individual conscience and knowledge and obligation, have been advocates of the necessity of fighting evil with knowledge. The Adult Schools of the early nineteenth century drew their force from a zeal, both religious and social, to teach the scriptures to the poor. They did this perhaps with mixed motives; but they established the important educational fact that adults could learn.[2]

These religious origins did much to associate adult education both with social needs and, at the same time, the lonely individual quest of knowledge and truth. Adult education was born from the conflict of divided purpose. It was to remain subject to social tests of its usefulness and yet, in its character, retain dominant traits of an individual nature which would reject social measurements of its value, in the same way in which one would defy a government which sought to define truth. From the very beginning the function of adult learning was left undecided between quantitative and qualitative judgements.

It was, however, from the secular impulses of the industrial age that organised adult education received its chief direction and definition. In the eighteenth century the growth of clubs, the increased circulation of newspapers and periodicals, the popularity of circulating libraries, the enterprise of literary, musical, scientific and antiquarian societies began to shape the leisure of both the landed gentry and the rising commercial and professional classes. In the nineteenth century these secular interests broadened in both scope and influence to include the skilled workers and craftsmen of the growing industrial society. Mechanics' Institutes became the focus of this development.

Some were created by patronage, by the reforming zeal of middle-class radicals and others were the product, like that at Glasgow, of the efforts of working men themselves. Like the later Adult Schools there were mixed motives and different expectations. Self-improvement, the use of knowledge to change the individual's place in society, the pure search for facts and understanding, and the demand for political change were all major drives. Within the great variety of foundations and in the light of their varying histories it is not easy to select an overall characteristic of this movement. It is, however, largely true that the emphasis of this adult learning was upon factual knowledge rather than cultural enrichment.

Developments in the nineteenth century had once more made it clear that, while the support for and the strength of adult education was to be largely determined by social estimates, the fact that it was for adults would inevitably give it marked individual variety. For the adult, however uneducated, will have some experience of living which will provide an ability to test educational satisfaction. Moreover, once again it had been shown that adult learning could take place even in the most difficult conditions.

The industrial society of the nineteenth century provided for the educational needs of the adult in many ways and through many institutions whose main objects were not educational. The Co-operative movement, the Trade Unions, the political clubs and associations and Chartist movement, the agricultural societies and the reading rooms were all concerned. This variety represented, however, not simply differences in activity but in purpose. It is indeed evidence of the vigour of the nineteenth century and an important reminder of the educational capacities of the adult. It is a variety which can be seen as both functional and organic. It confirms what has been already observed, namely that through all the declared social purposes remains the individual's own test of his educational demands as an adult. Even when adult education is written into the programme of a political party the final test remains individual. The choice to continue to be educated remains voluntary in adult life.

The peak of the varied adult education activities of the nineteenth century was reached as a result of the contributions of the Adult Schools, Working Men's clubs and colleges, with the greater participation of the universities. It is nevertheless important that this contribution, however distinctive, could only take place against this variety of needs and purposes which had given such strong individual characteristics to adult learning.

University activity in adult education represented fundamentally an extension of higher learning associated with the increase in the number of universities themselves. It was a situation which with modifications could perhaps be found again today. The second half of the nineteenth century saw the growth of institutions of higher learning in the provinces; the second half of this century has entered into another major institutional expansion of higher education. In the nineteenth century this growth was associated with the needs of adults; today the rapidly changing character of knowledge and the inherited pressures of the exclusion of many from university education could again produce a major growth of courses of higher education for the adult.

It would still remain true that possible contemporary developments, with whatever degree of skill they were to avail themselves of new methods of communication and techniques of learning with television and mechanical aids, would have to take note of the character of adult learning given it by the conditions of historical growth.

This need for adaptation to the circumstances of adults can be seen in the direction of university extension work from the late 1870's. Guided reading and instruction through lecturing became married to the established adult notion and practice of discussion and argument. The teacher's conception of a formal syllabus and the often unschooled queries of the adult mind had each to make concessions to what could constitute successful communication in practice.

The main influence of the universities was to inform the liberal and humane spirit of adult education with the standards of scholarship, although it is necessary to remember that the Extension movement of the 1880's and 1890's did not neglect either technical courses nor plainly vocational ones often linked with teacher training and the need for adults to gain certificates to proceed to further examinations. University adult teaching set a conception of academic standards difficult to define but recognisable to the student as intrinsic in the whole nature of study. It did this most effectively when in close association with expressed adult needs, and such a formal co-operation of an academic approach to learning with the realities of the adult world was achieved in the tutorial classes arranged jointly with the Workers' Educational Association.

This association of students, founded in 1903, gathered together many of the historical strands in adult education and sought to match them to the needs of the industrial democracy of the early twentieth century. The early religious emphasis on the obligation to learn was there even if the movement, in order to provide as wide a base as possible, stresses its non-sectarian character. The radical inspirations of a hundred years earlier were recognisable in new political clothing even if the movement was non-party political. This was a nineteenth century culmination. It was education for adults consciously aware of the need for democratic action to be enlightened by knowledge and shaped by wisdom: it was adult learning also widely aware of the pleasures of study divorced from political or social action.

The phase beginning in 1906 of sustained co-operation between university extra-mural teaching and the Workers' Educational Association, symbolised by the work of the tutorial classes of a three years' period of study, was interrupted by the First World War although the organisation of the W.E.A. was in fact stronger in 1918 than it had been in 1913.[3] It is a co-operation which still exists, although to-day it has to some extent lost its central place in the planning of extra-mural work. It was as much culmination of earlier developments as it was the beginning of a decisive new phase. It is for this reason that there has been so much discussion, especially since 1945, as to whether these nineteenth century assumptions of the immediacy of the link between knowledge and action and of the self-evident good of the humanist's faith, which are contained in this approach to adult learning, can continue to be held as central to our thinking now.

There is no answer to this question which can be wrested from the statistics of adult classes today. The factors which determine the adult's choice in education and indeed his decision as to whether he will seek formal assistance at all are not wholly known, and they are above all operative within only the known availabilities.

What can be said is that, whatever policies are to be shaped today in adult education, the historical antecedents, even so briefly described as they are here, will continue to influence both the methods of the teacher and the expectations of the student, and that changes will have to be made with this situation in mind.

2. TUTOR, STUDENT, AND SUBJECT

The main historical trends described have influenced the teacher in university extra-mural work chiefly in his identification of his rôle as a tutor. This point is made frequently by the writers of this book whatever their teaching subject. The religious stress on conscience, the reformist emphasis on purpose, the academic insistence on tolerance of view all come together in this form of adult education to mean that didacticism is out of place. Teaching becomes inseparable from the demand which any individual has the right to make that the subject be made relevant to his adult needs. The subject must remain "open". It is an education in which relationships within knowledge, however much they slip and fall from the definition of "subject", are perhaps more important than anything else.

The adult student too is often a product of these attitudes. Few adults will in fact approach formal education with a clear-cut set of requirements about the way in which they should be taught. They are in many circumstances likely to have no interest in the distinctive factors which have shaped the character of extra-mural teaching. However, the simple fact that, whatever their motive in seeking education, they will bring into the class a variety of considerations and conclusions about man and God and society will mean that frequently, although certainly not inevitably, the test of learning will be mature. The question "why?" and "how?" will remain at the centre of the process of adult learning.

It is clear from the following chapters that this "open" nature of adult education is not equally the case in every subject. The teaching of science, for example, to adults has not, as might have been supposed, met with a consistent demand that the fundamental nature of scientific thinking should be analysed nor that the social and moral implications of scientific knowledge should be examined. It has been found that there is rather a wish to learn a particular aspect of a particular science. It is not the history nor the philosophy of science which is demanded so much as a real participation in some part of its actuality. This is perhaps not so surprising. It is, after all, how the scientist himself works. The discussion of implication is more likely to arise at a later stage: certainly even within the process of study of a science the adult will not refrain from asking the general question carrying widespread implications when the study suggests that it should be asked.

In the visual arts and in music the writers show how the adult again determines the way in which theories of a subject and traditional scales of priorities have to be moulded to his individual needs. In these subjects it is certain that it is impossible to maintain any strict dividing line between theoretical structures and the need to associate knowledge with the test and revelation of practice. The wide freedom enjoyed in the teaching of the adult, which is the legacy of the past, means today as it always did that the adult student constantly re-interprets the significance of knowledge in the conditions of the contemporary world.

This kind of freedom remains at the centre of things. It is not a product of a particular administrative arrangement in extra-mural work. It has been claimed by many that the social changes which have taken place since 1945 have had their consequences for adult education. It is said that a good deal of the pre-war edge of discontent has gone; knowledge as a conscious instrument of political direction has now more complicated innuendoes;

personal demands for the use of leisure are more in evidence than group demands for guidance to action; increased leisure, longer retirement, mass communication in entertainment and instruction have all tended to merge adult learning with an amorphous cultural complexion. Yet at no time has university extra-mural work lost its freedom to respond to indications of changed adult need however cautious it is about the way in which the new demands can be satisfactorily squared with academic requirements.

It is especially within this area of inherited freedom that adult learning develops its own special characteristics. Those who write in this book about those subjects which can by their nature be considered as organic in adult society, chiefly economics and politics, are concerned to point out that with the adult there will always be both a demand to stretch a study so that it illuminates and to concentrate it on occasion so that its methods are revealed. This is, perhaps, especially true of the teaching of history.

The more one steps into the experience of adult teachers over a range of subjects the more are two main propositions about adult learning emphasised. First, that each teaching scheme, at the outset determined by sequences within the subject, has to be modified; secondly, that because the scope of adult experience is wide and sometimes sharply relevant there is constant room for experiment in teaching.

The characteristics of extra-mural work are thus not determined by a testament. The historical influences are not restrictive practices associated with one set of circumstances and consequently made suddenly inappropriate by changes in social structure. At every historical stage there have been changes in the subjects and shifts in the administrative and organisational pattern. These will continue. The historical legacy is, in its culmination, a simple recognition that the adult has to be taught in freedom.

It is for this reason that many of the changes which it is possible to anticipate as likely to take place within the next decade can be looked at with a reasonable confidence that they will be effectively carried through. All the exciting possibilities of a "University of the Air" will still mean that the nature of the subject and the selected reading requirements for any sustained study will have to be geared to adult attitudes to learning if they are to be effective.

The possibilities that more adult students will wish their learning to be recognised by examination and certificate need not be seen as upsetting a tradition without the support of which the values of disinterested study will collapse. If the freedom of teaching is maintained there seems no reason why experiments with courses which would meet both demands should not be successful. After all, in any form of adult teaching beyond the plainly and exclusively vocational, the motives of the student and his expectations are widely different in any single class.

What is said about language teaching in this book is relevant. There is no doubt that for many adults the motive in learning a foreign language is to acquire a skill and they wish to see their ability to do so tested and recognised: it is hardly possible otherwise to gain the evidence with which to direct their study. At the same time, this need not exclude an entry for them through language into literary and historical studies. Adult teaching is not unitary; it can be directed if need be by practical and even vocational considerations without surrendering the freedom to range. It might even be argued that one of the basic social purposes of adult education is to break down the notion of compartments in knowledge and the assumption that there are stratifications of value in the considerations which lead adults to different selections in study. Adults live all the time making infinitely different kinds of choice; these choices interlock in any individual life. Adult education has to cater for the certainty that adults will change their views about their purposes in learning as part of that learning itself.

Ideally, adult education should take place in conditions where, under one roof, it would be possible for a wide variety of types of course and selection of subject to co-exist alongside the social amenities which would encourage people to meet and talk. Only on a small scale has it ever been possible to arrange this, and sometimes it has been pursued as a sort of missionary policy to close the supposed gaps between the people who choose a subject of disinterested study and those who opt for a vocational end. It has been advocated as though a bridge were to be built between two cultures. In fact, the people who might study literature and those who, for example, seek to bring their mathematics up to date, and those who perhaps as social workers join a class studying principles of administration, turn out to be the same kind of people. It has not indeed often occurred to the adult student that his choice can be considered so differentiating a factor in his approach to knowledge: and he is right. It ought not to be.

3. ADMINISTRATIVE RÔLES AND CONSEQUENCES

Administrative arrangements in the "provision" of adult education have also had some effect in sharpening differences between one kind of course and another. It is fortunate that in this respect administrative practice has not been uniform and therefore comparisons can be made.

It has been shown how university extra-mural work grew from the voluntary efforts of the nineteenth century. The local education authority had hardly any concern with the education of adults until the Education Act of 1902. Gradually their rôle became greater. Not only did they provide premises and make grants to a number of voluntary bodies but they became themselves direct providers on a large scale and were plainly given the responsibility by the 1944 Education Act. In England and Wales the special characteristics of the universities and the Workers' Educational Association among other bodies were recognised and they became "Responsible Bodies" eligible for direct financial grant from the Ministry of Education. In Scotland the local authority uses the University Extra-Mural Committees as agents in the provision of a comprehensive educational service for adults.

The difference is not simply an administrative one. It has a significance in the whole question of the definition and determination of the categories in adult education and the function of university extra-mural work. In England and Wales the tendency has been for the division of labour between the local authority and the university extra-mural department to be largely a subject division. Vocational and craft subjects were the province of the local authority; the "liberal studies" were the province of the university. This division has never been absolute. The work of the local authority evening institutes has always covered many of the liberal subjects; the changing nature of university courses in social studies, administration, and applied science has inevitably meant that university extra-mural work reflecting this change has been able to give to adults courses much in demand but clearly possessed of at the least a semi-vocational character. The expansion of technical colleges and colleges of advanced technology with their accompanying growth of General Studies departments has also meant a blurring of the division of responsibility.

It is not that it is impossible to define the qualities which should be uniquely characteristic of university extra-mural teaching: but it is certainly not possible to rest the function of university work in adult education upon an administrative structure confusedly associated with subject definitions. Such a statement as "The universities as teaching institutions have a special responsibility for making available to all who are capable of receiving it such teaching as falls within their province, at the quality which is proper to a university. They should not be called upon to teach outside their walls subjects which do not and cannot properly fall within the internal university curriculum"[4] implies an unexceptionable standard of university quality and yet fundamentally begs the question of what should be taught. Since this was written in 1958 universities both new and old have made many changes in curriculum. Robert Peers continued: "For the mainly recreative activities which are now generally, if somewhat confusingly, described as adult education, local education authorities where they exist are the most appropriate agencies." It is certainly true that there are many adult recreations which could not conceivably be considered as proper activities for university teaching, but no division which left these as the sphere of a local authority and thought of university work with adults as wholly non-recreational would now be possible.

It is noteworthy that this kind of customary division of function between local authority and university issued in an almost complete prohibition on the universities in the teaching of foreign languages to adults. If there is a pre-supposition that there are easily discernible levels of teaching to adults then it is easy to conclude that a university ought only to teach language to those who already possess at least the rudiments of knowledge. If university extra-mural work is defined as wholly non-vocational, then it can be held that, since for many adults the learning of a second language will be practical in aim, such an engagement is inappropriate. However, since adults do want to learn languages and since many do prefer the kind of way in which university extra-mural courses are conducted to other forms of further education, university departments in England and Wales have to try to bend the regulations to meet this need. Above all, this approach to subject and motive in adult learning ignores altogether one important point of view. Many university teachers of language believe that language can be best taught from the beginning by the university, and that adult education in this respect offers a welcome opportunity.

In Scotland where, as has been said, the university in its extra-mural work is more closely associated with the local authority, it is easier to avoid some of these uneasy distinctions of provision. It is true that, since its finances do not come from a central source but from the local authorities themselves as payment for services rendered, a Scottish university extra-mural department has probably less freedom in its planning of courses, and its policy will have to be measured to varying demands from several authorities with widely differing views about adult education. At the same time it will be at the centre of things with each education authority and thus not duplicate what can be provided by the authorities themselves. Nor is its freedom to decide on the nature of its classes impaired even if in the conduct of them, in respect for example of minimum numbers, it is more closely bound to local education committee further education regulations and practices.

Great Britain is at the beginning of a decisive phase of expansion of higher education, and this has already made and will make increasingly in the future for changes in the outlook and design of adult education. The demand for a wide variety of specialised courses to meet the rapid advances in knowledge is now generally recognised. The need for specialists, whose own education and work is so narrowly confined, to use adult education as an enlarging and liberating influence has registered itself already in the considerable number of scientists and technologists who study the arts in established adult life and, to a lesser degree, the arts men who, aware of their ignorance of the omnipresent scientific environment, seek to correct this through adult education. In this expansion local authorities will have a determining influence and it is likely that the whole notion of the education of adults will be revised in that the provision made will be regularised in a wide-spread service in which the links between further education and school and college and university will be formally established. If it is, then it seems inevitable that in England and Wales university extra-mural work will have to have much closer relations with the local authorities than is at present the case, and that in Scotland there will need to be a further definition of the particular function of extra-mural work within the scope of local authority provision.

The chief feature of adult education in Great Britain has been its variety and the multiplicity of bodies concerned with it. This is partly a result of history and partly an indication of varied group needs expressed through voluntary agencies. Most university extra-mural teachers have welcomed this variety partly because it gave them freedom and to a degree defined their scope: many have accepted it because any centralisation seemed unworkable and, other things being equal, undesirable. It is doubtful, however, whether all the duplications can survive, and not all priorities have proper breathing space in the present system, where what is done is in part determined by whether public funds can be gained to support it and partly in ignorance of what others may be planning.

4.   RESOURCES AND TASKS FOR THE FUTURE

These questions of administrative practice are inseparable from the discussion of adult teaching in the following chapters. An expansion of adult education means a demand for more teachers; any further regularisation of the education of adults is likely to entail consideration of the proper qualifications and working conditions of further education teachers. University extra-mural departments have for some time carried out short courses in the training of tutors and some have systematised this with a diploma or certificate. For the most part, however, the view has been held that a good adult tutor is born not made, that experience alone can improve technique.

It would appear from what follows in this book that there are many special characteristics in adult learning. The approaches to subject can be defined; particular arts of teaching can be des-cribed: especially suitable types of teaching aid and demonstration can be listed. There is in the history of adult education much which can be learnt about adult attitudes which vitally affect our approaches today. There are varieties of practice in the organisation of adult education which can be studied, analysed and compared. There are some ways of teaching, in fact, and some methods of organisation which are better than others. This can all be taught and before too long it will become necessary to decide how the training of teachers for adults is to be carried out and by whom. If it is not anticipated it will happen *ad hoc* and nobody will be satisfied.

There are also likely to be developments in the teaching of adults within industry. Some of this is already done on a small scale by extra-mural departments and the W.E.A., some by the Trade Unions and employers. Whatever doubts there may be about whether the factory is a suitable venue for education, whatever uncertainties there may be about the wisdom of treating an adult *qua* worker or *qua* trade unionist, however much it may be an educational truism that it is preferable for the adult to regard himself simply as a member of a mixed adult group rather than as an industrial function, it seems certain that there will have to be more courses than there are now consciously planned for the industrial workers at all levels. The T.U.C. has recognised this as have many firms themselves. It is by no means clear yet how it can best be done, but it will certainly in another form raise the question of what is the appropriate training for those who teach adults.

There are, further, new needs in industrial training which will involve adult education methods. Automation produces rapidly changing job-situations in which re-training for a new task has to be undertaken at perhaps a fairly advanced stage in adult life. Some of this necessary mobility in jobs can perhaps be anticipated even as early as the apprenticeship period but not all, as forecasts of the precise effects of automation in a particular industry are difficult. Nor is this problem confined to the industrial worker whose job is overtaken by a machine process: there are managers, industrial scientists and researchers all of whom could be re-deployed to advantage if proper educational programmes were devised. These are perhaps not tasks in which university extra-mural departments could play a major part, but they are necessary provisions which will have to make use of adult education techniques and experience.

Experience of both teaching adults and of learning as adults is more widespread than supposed. There is a considerable turnover of adult students. A Glasgow calculation would indicate that, over any period of five years, there will be in the region of three times the number of students who will at some point have attended a course as are constituted in any single annual total. If this could be regarded as typical then over a decade as much as one ninth of the adult population might be estimated as having made some contact with formal organised adult education. The turn-over of teachers is less marked partly because those engaged full-time are few and most of them appointed in the last twelve years. But their numbers are small as a proportion of the total. It is known, moreover, that among university teachers there is a tendency to act as part-time extra-mural tutors during earlier years of appointment. The number of professors and senior lecturers who take part is comparatively small. During the last three years' period in the teaching of Glasgow University Extra-Mural Department one sixth of the total teaching was carried out by new annual entrants. Constant recruitment and annual loss of tutors at an age when many have fifteen or more years of internal work left does mean that at any time there is greater experience of adult teaching than is actively used. This widespread experience of both student and tutor could possibly be gathered and used more than it is as part of the necessary material for any co-ordinated scheme of training and study of methods. Above all, the changing personnel of teachers emphasises how necessary it is that the acquisition of adult education teaching techniques is not left to chance and slow accumulation of experience. By the time a part-time tutor has learnt the skills he has probably reached the end of his spell at the work.

It has been recognised by the Ministry of Education that a proper use of full-time staff in adult education is the training of part-time teachers. This recognition can be regarded as part of the much wider problem of the nature of adult teaching as a profession and permanent career.[5] The changing needs of adult education alter the kind of qualifications required in full-time staff. In university extra-mural work the chief criterion has been academic but, as it is hardly ever possible to make a complete separation between teaching and rudimentary organising and administration in adult education, additional qualities have been demanded of staff. In any case, teaching adults demands a flexibility of approach and a sustained interest in teaching itself beyond that normally sought from an internal university teacher.

These selection criteria are bound to be modified. The growth of specialised courses means that the teaching for these will have to be carried out almost entirely by internal university teachers, or that full-time extra-mural staff will have to be allowed themselves to specialise more than they do now and at the price of serving fewer functions. Internal teaching resources in the universities are already heavily committed and it would be unwise to believe that the new needs of adult students can be met by the willingness of university staff to take on this extra work even if they are prepared to recognise its importance. Need in the field of adult education has tended to outstrip provision for a long time. It may be cheaper to meet increased demand by the employment of part-time teaching resources, but all the requirements of a full-time educational service for adults can only be met by an increase in the number of full-time engagements. And that will mean that conditions of professional employment and promotion prospects in both local authority work and in the university extra-mural departments will have to be related and regularised.

Adult education today could be at the beginning of a major development. Whatever shape it takes and whatever priorities government and public demand establish for it, the experience of those who have taught will be relevant to what can be done. It is hoped that the accumulation of experience contained in the succeeding chapters will provide a guide to all who might enter this exciting sector of education. Whatever patterns emerge and however the work is divided it will be impossible to ignore the past: there has been adult education of one kind or another long enough for some tradition to have weight. In the world of university extra-mural work, freedom to dispute must remain paramount whatever specialised tasks are undertaken. The adult will never see education as knowledge alone. There will always be dissent in society and when that dissent is able to change things for the better it will be because of the educated adult.

Adult education is today determined by the broad educational needs of society as much as it was in the eighteenth and nineteenth centuries. Those needs are indisputably marked by both earlier deficiencies in provision for secondary school and present inadequacies in the universities. The age groups in adult students span a long series of gaps from primary to higher education. It must have the resources to work at many levels to meet many needs. In all its variety, however, those who teach will always have to be aware of the kind of conditions of practice described in this book.

This generalised account of the growth of adult education, and tentative estimate of the directions in which it is likely to develop in the future, can perhaps be best seen in perspective against the actuality of the extra-mural provision of a single university. This might serve to emphasise also that those who write about their approaches to particular subjects do so from within the context of a particular programme. It is true, however, that what is done by the University of Glasgow both in urban and rural areas has many points of comparison with general practice in both England and Wales.

Details, therefore, about range of subjects in extra-mural work and other information on the educational and occupational background of adult students and tutors are given in an appendix.

NOTES TO CHAPTER I

[1] THOMAS KELLY, *A History of Adult Education in Great Britain* (1962).

[2] ROBERT PEERS, *Adult Education. A Comparative Study* (1958), p. 12.

[3] T. KELLY, *op. cit.*, p. 257.

[4] R. PEERS, *op. cit.*, p. 349.

[5] *Adult Educ.*, **XXXV**, 5 (January, 1963), for general views of problem of staffing.

CHAPTER II

ARCHAEOLOGY

J. X. W. P. Corcoran

BY THE early years of this decade it appeared that the great demand for adult classes in archaeology, which developed rapidly in the years following the 1939-45 War, was already declining. For many of those concerned with the provision of classes, tutors and administrators alike, this was a relief in that the supply of suitable tutors during that period was rarely adequate to meet demand. This does not imply either that demand has ceased or that archaeology will tend to disappear from adult education programmes. On the contrary, archaeology has now acquired in some areas of Britain a status comparable with that enjoyed by subjects considered as traditional within adult education. Demand for such classes at the present time differs from that of the fifties in that the former is perhaps more commonly based on a serious demand for knowledge of archaeology. This is not meant to imply that earlier demand was of a frivolous nature but annual reports of extra-mural departments and W.E.A. district offices showed that in many areas classes in archaeology seldom extended beyond a terminal or introductory course. There were many reasons for this, some of which remain valid today, and they are discussed in this chapter.

It seems probable that the two successful television series, *Animal, Vegetable or Mineral?* and *Buried Treasure* stimulated an interest which was only indirectly beneficial to archaeology and adult education. There is little doubt of their success as entertainment but few archaeologists, whether or not associated with adult classes, would consider that the first series ever reached the level of *haute vulgarisation* occasionally attained by the second. This is not intended as an indictment of BBC television educational policy for it is obvious that these programmes were intended to "instruct" only as an incidental to entertainment. They are not to be compared, for example, with the Third Network

sound radio series, *The Archaeologist*. Specific reference is made to
these television series because they stimulated a demand for
classes in archaeology which could not always be met, primarily
because of lack of suitable tutors. It is perhaps significant that
since the completion of the series demand for appropriate classes
has lessened. This illustrates one type of motive which has influenced and will undoubtedly continue to influence potential
adult students in all subjects.

In addition to a demand fostered by glamorous presentation of a
subject in a variety of media, there is a smaller but more constant
demand for classes in archaeology which is closely allied to the
history of the study of the subject in Britain. Until the present
century archaeological research was conducted mainly by ama-
teurs, as few archaeologists were professionally employed. The
position is changing rapidly, not so much because of any great
proliferation in the number of professional archaeologists, but
because only full-time archaeologists can attempt to keep abreast
of the rapid developments in their own branch of the subject and
relate them to the general archaeological background. This does
not imply that there is no place for the amateur. On the contrary,
current archaeological research demands the accumulation of
detailed data from which to produce syntheses and it is here that
the amateur archaeologist is able to contribute his specialised
knowledge.   The strongly amateur and local bias of archaeology
in Britain has a long history of development from the sixteenth
century, and the continued importance of the amateur's rôle today
is one of the pleasing aspects of the study in that professional and
amateur can frequently meet together on equal terms.

Intensified interest in antiquity dates from the Renaissance
when a strong sense of nationalism fostered interest in the native
past. In the eighteenth century it was common for young noblemen
to be taken, as part of their education, on the Grand Tour by their
tutors to visit the more impressive remains of the classical past in
Mediterranean lands. On their return to Britain, sometimes to
estates which contained prehistoric, Roman or later monuments,
they began to interest themselves in British antiquities. Normally
this was directed in the main to the acquisition of artifacts to add
to their "cabinets of curios", a collection perhaps originating in
objects acquired on the Grand Tour. Unfortunately, this led to

widespread excavation of which the sole end was usually the discovery of artifacts and nothing else.

With the Romantic Revival interest in the past was widened. The Industrial Revolution produced a new educated middle-class which became identified with the traditional squirearchy and the clergy of the established church. As far as archaeology was concerned the most important development was the formation of local county archaeological societies, many of which were founded in the middle of the last century and continue to flourish. Attitudes to archaeology continued to bear that stamp of dilettantism which had typified those of the previous century. There were, however, two important differences. One was the publication by societies of journals which meant that information was readily exchanged. The second was the formation of county museums, often based on the private collections of members.

Although excavation continued at a rate which would not be tolerated today, it was accompanied by a growing realisation that it was possible to learn about the past from a study of field-monuments and their artifacts. Collecting as such became less important. These developments contributed to the creation of governmental agencies concerned with antiquities and the slow introduction into universities of British archaeological studies.

It is important to appreciate the history of the development of archaeology in Britain and in particular the strength of archaeological societies. The latter are in a sense providing adult education for their members, or at least making available through their programme of lectures and by their publications some of the results of latest research. There are close links between some societies and certain extra-mural departments, links which are of considerable value to both.

The student who is also a member of an archaeological society, who perhaps has a detailed knowledge of his local archaeology, differs considerably from one who may not have any previous knowledge of the subject and who has been attracted to an adult class by a television programme or popular book. These types of student may represent only two of a wide range who may differ, not only in their variable knowledge of archaeology, but also in age and intelligence and in extreme diversity of educational background. The tutor, however, may meet the class for six, twelve or twenty-four weeks or even for three or four years, and the differing needs of each student will have to be satisfied. It may be asked how can a tutor plan a syllabus which will accomplish it.

This is a problem which is common to liberal adult education as a whole, but in certain respects archaeology enjoys some advantages. It is a truism that teaching non-vocational subjects to adults in university extra-mural and W.E.A. classes differs from teaching either school children or internal university students. These differences arise from a variety of reasons and, in general, a discussion of them is relevant to the teaching of any non-vocational subject. Archaeology is in a somewhat special position for as a subject it is taught in Britain more widely in adult classes than in either schools or universities. Admittedly, most school children are taught some prehistory, usually in junior forms, and from there progress to some acquaintance with the literate ancient world represented by Greece and Rome. They may learn something of Ancient Egypt and Mesopotamia and possibly something of the archaeological background to the Old Testament. Archaeology as a subject in its own right, however, is not normally taught. Within universities the teaching of archaeology is a relatively new development, few universities having independent departments and those mostly small.

These factors have an important bearing on teaching archaeology to adults. In the first place, most adult students of whatever academic background are unlikely to have been systematically taught the subject in the past and they are therefore normally unlikely to have to make any of the intellectual adjustments which might be necessary in the case of, say, history or literature. Again, there is no long-established tradition of teaching archaeology in any form which might assist or hinder a tutor new to adult education. Finally, because of restricted teaching in universities there are few fully qualified archaeologists available as tutors.

It may be accepted, then, that any class is likely to include students who have no previous knowledge of the subject whatever but who wish to acquire a fundamental grasp of whatever aspect of archaeology is the subject of the course. If the course is concerned with British archaeology some of those students may eventually wish to take part in excavation. The same class may also include a member of a local society who has a deep knowledge of his local archaeology, based on a close familiarity with the publications of that society which may comprise as many as a hundred annual volumes.

Archaeology may be defined as the study and interpretation of the material remains of the past. Emphasis is placed on material remains and for this reason the use of archaeological techniques is applied in varying degrees to the study of the historical period. This obvious fact is stated because in planning a class a tutor or organiser may be uncertain of the exact needs of a group requesting a class on archaeology. Frequently there is confusion between archaeology and prehistory and many assume that the two are synonymous. Whereas archaeological techniques may be applied to the study of historic times up to periods as recent as the nineteenth century A.D. in the recently defined branch of Industrial Archaeology, prehistory is concerned only with the period of man's emergence and development before the local use of written records. The latter is therefore the study of by far the greatest part of man's existence, the beginnings of which may date to one million or more years ago. Nowhere in the world has the local historic period yet extended over a duration of more than five thousand years and some regions are in the twentieth century only now emerging from their prehistory.

A class in archaeology may therefore study any period in any part of the world from the first beginnings of human activity in that area to the present century, based on a consideration of material remains. Theoretically, objects which have just become obsolescent qualify under the heading of "material remains of the past". In this sense the present interest in, for example, veteran motor-cars and tramcars is properly an archaeological study. If this seems an excessive claim it is supported by the collections of such objects which many museums are at present building. What may appear merely as a "bygone" today will be a true artifact of the distant past five hundred years or a millennium hence. Industrial Archaeology has developed from the need to record and preserve specific examples of machinery and buildings dating from the period of the Industrial Revolution in Britain. This has been shown to be necessary because their proximity in time to the present century has tended to obscure their importance within the history of technology. Absence of adequate written records has necessitated the use of purely archaeological techniques in dating structures such as some of the earliest iron-framed buildings.

It may seem that discussion of Industrial Archaeology is remote from the theme of this chapter but the subject has already appeared in syllabuses of adult classes, and indeed the rapid recognition of its importance has in part been achieved by the active work of extra-mural tutors. Although archaeological techniques may be used in an industrial context, they form only one of several disciplines which include local, national and economic history, economics, sociology and geology. In this, Industrial Archaeology resembles the archaeological content of the study of other historic periods.

Mediaeval Archaeology is now also an accepted academic discipline in its own right with professional archaeologists holding university posts. In Britain its time-range extends from the end of the Roman occupation to the beginnings of the modern Period. Although much contemporary documentary evidence has survived from this millennium or so, the use of archaeological techniques has recently provided greatly increased knowledge of many aspects of mediaeval life, including problems concerned with Anglo-Saxon immigration and settlement, early development of castle architecture and the deserted villages of England.

Industrial Archaeology and Mediaeval Archaeology are two relatively new branches of the study of the material remains of the past. Classical Archaeology is one of the oldest and, like the study of the archaeology of the Near East, contributes an important part of knowledge of these ancient civilisations. Beyond these in time is prehistory, and here archaeology and its associated disciplines alone have to be used, without the aid of written records, in any attempt to learn about that lengthy and formative period of man's past.

Even within a restricted part of the Old World, then, there are several self-contained archaeological disciplines. Reference to Africa, India, Asia and the Americas would add more. The majority of adult classes usually study one of these with particular emphasis on Prehistoric and Roman Britain and the Anglo-Saxons, although almost every aspect of archaeological study, whether in the Old World or in the New, has probably been discussed in one adult class or another in Britain since 1945. Tutors in other disciplines, such as history or anthropology, may feel that tutors in archaeology are not keeping within their limits in organising classes in Mediaeval or Industrial Archaeology or in the Prehistory of Africa. Certainly it is difficult to draw any well-defined demarcation line between subjects appropriate to these and other disciplines, but it is one of the strengths and joys of adult education that the conventional academic boundaries need not be observed.

Although there may be much variety within archaeological studies generally, the one unifying factor is the emphasis on the study and interpretation of the material remains of the past. Here lies the unity of the basic techniques which may include an iron-framed mill in Derbyshire, broken potsherds from Troy, Stonehenge, the French Palaeolithic caves and the Parthenon. It is here that the student may receive his first intellectual surprise and his reaction to it may condition the whole of his subsequent study or rejection of archaeology as a proper subject of study. A student coming for the first time to a class in history will have little difficulty in accepting the discipline of historic studies and will probably have had some experience of studying history, no matter at how low a level. The long tradition of history classes in adult education is part proof of this. Once the student can grasp the essential fact that prehistoric potsherds, stones, bones or pieces of corroded metal themselves are not important as much as the interpretation which may be derived from study of them, then the first stage of the acceptance of archaeological evidence as a proper tool of historical research, in its widest sense, has been reached.

In its broadest aspects archaeology may offer mental training of the radical sort, and sometimes the intellectual excitement, which have long remained part of the tradition of liberal adult education. No matter what aspect of the subject is studied, a tutor should attempt to present the basic evidence and to demonstrate how an interpretation of the material remains can contribute to an understanding of what was happening in the past. This is particularly relevant in prehistoric studies where many examples can be given of how it is possible to build up a picture of life during different periods of prehistory in different parts of the world from a study of related field-monuments and associated artifacts derived from them. A similar exercise may also be attempted using archaeological material relating to historical periods by demonstrating how archaeological material may assist in supplying evidence which is lacking in documentary sources. By so doing, training in the fundamentals of archaeological thought is being given.

These fundamentals should underly any teaching in archaeology. In practice, however, emphasis is naturally placed on the more specific problems connected with the study of a particular period or region. It is here that the practical difficulties in presenting his material will face the tutor. The university lecturer in archaeology is normally fortunate in having at his disposal a collection of visual aids without which the subject cannot be adequately taught. He will also have access to essential published material. The internal student will have the advantage of similar benefits. In practice it is rare that either tutor or student in adult classes will have comparable facilities and this is one of the problems most difficult of solution, although fundamentally it is merely one of financial provision.

The visual content of archaeological material is important both in teaching and in learning, as it is in the appreciation of art. General problems may be discussed without such aids but detailed study of fundamental techniques such as typology is impossible. The blackboard is perhaps not used as much as it might be, as many tutors underestimate their ability to draw simple diagrams. Photographs which can be passed around the class may be useful, but they tend to hold up the pace of the class to such an extent that some members of the class may be looking at illustrations relevant to points made by the tutor five or ten minutes earlier. The epidiascope is valuable if it is an efficient machine and the tutor can master the intricacies of feeding it illustrations of different sizes and composition.

The slide projector is undoubtedly the most efficient instrument, but its use may involve the tutor in considerable difficulties in obtaining sufficient slides. This is primarily a matter of finance, complicated by the essentially idiosyncratic choice of material by any archaeologist in planning a slide collection. As far as adult education is concerned the ideal would be a personal collection for each tutor, but this is generally impracticable. The alternative would be a slide collection held by an extra-mural department on which all tutors could draw. Again there would be considerable difficulties in administering it, unless the initial grant made to finance it was sufficiently large both to make it as comprehensive as possible and to enable a large number of duplicate slides to be made at the outset. Duplicates would be essential as several tutors taking courses on similar subjects would be drawing on it simultaneously. For tutors living some distance from the department there would be the considerable difficulty of selection and the added administrative complication of dispatching slides through the post. Furthermore, it would not always be possible to maintain a strict schedule of borrowing as adult education allows the welcome flexibility of not maintaining strict adherence to a syllabus. Tutors of all subjects will recognise that it is common not to complete discussion in any one meeting of material planned for that evening. It would be an added difficulty if slides were lent to individual tutors for a fixed and limited period.

There is often a tendency among tutors to use too many slides in any single meeting. This often prevents slides from remaining sufficiently long on the screen. Students new to archaeology are unfamiliar with archaeological material and they may not initially be able to interpret even a simple site-plan or conventional pottery drawings. In this connection, too, tutors sometimes overlook the need of students to take notes or to make drawings. Wherever possible the room should not be completely darkened or, if this is impossible, a limit should be set on the time during which the room is blacked-out.

The most important visual aid is undoubtedly an artifact of the period under discussion. Whereas in an ideal world a tutor might expect to receive some official assistance in the provision of slides, he may reasonably be expected to use his own initiative in borrowing a small teaching collection. Many museum curators, particularly those of local museums, will arrange the loan of such a collection. This, of course, will normally be of use to tutors taking classes in British Archaeology, and particularly those concentrating on local antiquities. This may be supplemented by visits to the museums themselves where students may be given the opportunity of handling artifacts, but this will depend in

varying degrees on the relative proximity of museums to the
meeting-place of the class. The question of visits in general is
intimately connected with that of visits to archaeological sites.

It is possible to teach more in a single well-planned visit than
in six months' class work and the details learned may be better
retained in the students' memory. The ability of the tutor to
include visits is naturally conditioned by the proximity of museums
and sites and the provision of such as part of a course is always
bound to remain unequal within Britain. Certain areas, such as
Wiltshire, the Cotswolds, parts of Wales and Scotland, are rich
in field-monuments of different periods. A certain balance, however, is maintained in that rural areas may be richer in sites,
whereas towns may provide museums. In classes dealing with
archaeology other than British, visits to sites are obviously
impossible although in some areas museums may display collections relevant to the subject.

Any adult class beyond the simplest introductory course will
assume that students will wish to read the relevant literature.
Provision of books and archaeological periodicals poses a problem
as complex as that of providing visual aids. The present pace of
archaeological research is such that any general survey becomes
quickly outdated and the tutor will naturally wish to recommend
reading of the most recent current fact and opinion. The bulk of
this is contained in a wide range of national and local specialised
journals, many written in languages not normally taught at
present in schools in Britain. The provision of adequate sets of
such periodicals is a problem which many university libraries find
difficult to solve. University extra-mural departments can hardly
be expected to attempt a similar provision, even if money were
available. Classes held within reach of adequate libraries, university or public, are fortunate in that arrangements sometimes
may be made for adult students to consult and even to borrow
relevant books and journals dealing with British Archaeology.
An ideal situation is that of a class in a county town which is
allowed to meet in the Reference Room of the local library which
holds complete sets of the journals of the local and some neighbouring archaeological societies and perhaps of one or two of the
major national societies. Classes held in remote areas are in a more
difficult position.

Adequate textbooks are not plentiful, although the series *Ancient Peoples and Places*, published by Thames and Hudson[1], and books on archaeology published by Penguin Books are currently providing well-produced and relatively inexpensive digests of many periods and regions. It should not be beyond the resources of most extra-mural departments in England and Wales to provide adequate books of this type for the class-library and some departments are generous in such provision.

If it is possible for the book-box to include journals and excavation reports, the tutor should not be afraid of recommending them to the class. Guidance should be given on the selection of reading from any given book, and it cannot be assumed that all students will be able adequately to use the list of contents and the index. It must be remembered that adult education may still involve the teaching of how to study effectively. Constant guidance should be given, particularly in warning students from excessive reliance on early popular books on the subject which they may encounter.

The difficulties frequently experienced in putting students in touch with appropriate reading matter emphasises the necessity for the tutor to be as comprehensive as possible in the presentation of lecture material. Although he is unlikely to be successful, the tutor of an adult class in archaeology should aim at providing his students with visual aids and access to books and journals comparable with those offered to an undergraduate. In a three-year tutorial class the standard should be, and often is, that of internal university teaching and the adult student should, as far as possible, be given appropriate facilities for the study of the subject.

Beyond this point, however, comparisons between internal and extra-mural teaching cease. Reference has already been made to the possibility of variety in the composition of the average class, both in age, intelligence and educational background. This raises the problem of the pace of the class. If the tutor thinks in terms of his least intelligent student he may lose the more intelligent. If he aims to satisfy the needs of the intelligent the others may tend to flounder. Some mean should be attempted with special attention given to the exceptional at either extreme, although there should be no hint of favouritism. The over-confident and prominent class members should be subdued lest they tend to make the less forceful insufficiently confident to contribute to class discussion. The latter should be stimulated and encouraged.

In archaeology classes there are factors which may counteract possible wide variations in intelligence and education and these become prominent in discussion periods. In dealing with the material remains of the past the archaeologist is constantly touching on aspects of life in which a large number of people have some direct knowledge, frequently more pertinent to the point under discussion than that of the tutor. A tutor has only to speak in a country district on a subject such as the origins of farming or in an industrial area on Roman technology or building methods to discover how much he himself can learn from others' experience and knowledge. Discussion is invariably stimulating to the tutor as well as to the class, particularly in hearing new views on old problems. It is a vital teaching aid but it must be planned to a certain extent by careful choice of question and comment. Such discussion may also demonstrate the success or otherwise of the presentation of teaching material. Wherever discussion is relevant to the subject it should be allowed to continue, even at the expense of abandoning lecture material for that particular evening. These factors are of course relevant to any adult teaching but they have an added importance in archaeology as discussion can demonstrate more accurately than can a formal exposition the easily forgotten truth that the primary aim of the study is to learn about the way of life of past peoples.

Discussion is only part of the teaching process and it must be integrated with formal exposition on the part of the tutor. In the preparation of a syllabus the tutor has considerable freedom to experiment as he is not normally bound by the fixed aim of preparation for an examination. In Britain there is a tradition that the class and the tutor together determine the syllabus at the initial meeting. In starting a new class, the class will be largely governed by the tutor in their choice.

There is here a possible conflict. To what extent should the class be given the syllabus it asks for if it conflicts with the achievement of a balanced syllabus? This can be a real problem in tutorial classes. It does, nevertheless, allow for flexibility in teaching. The students are not working for an examination and the class may travel at a leisurely pace with ample time for discussion. In planning a syllabus it is better not to include too much, or if the tutor realises later that too much has been included then he may choose not to complete the syllabus. It is usually possible to plan another course during the following session. It is surely preferable for the class to acquire an accurate appreciation of a little than a vague smattering of a more extensive subject. In this context the tutor should aim to offer his students the opportunity of acquiring an accurate comprehension of the particular subject studied in addition to a sympathetic understanding of the physical and mental processes of archaeology. In planning his syllabus the tutor should remember that he is not restricted to conventional academic divisions. If necessary, and if the tutor is competent, the syllabus may include discussion of material derived from associated disciplines, such as philology, anthropology, history, and mythology.

The presentation of the syllabus must normally differ from that offered to internal university students. Undergraduates expect succinct presentation of information and many can assimilate any number of typologies and archaeological cultures and the like. They also have ample time and the facilities for reading and discussion among themselves. They are young and they are full-time students with an adequate and recently acquired schooling behind them. They realise too, that they must read widely and deeply, or fail their examinations.

Adult students have no ultimate aim in the classes under discussion. They generally expect and should be given a complete survey of the subject. A fifty-year-old bank clerk may not be able at first to assimilate typologies and cultures, or even see their relevance. Initially he may be less interested in *minutiae* but he will be interested in the "human angle". This need should be satisfied without prejudicing scholarship.

For example, in teaching Neolithic Britain it may be useful to build a picture of the economy of the Windmill Hill culture and then extend discussion to secondary Neolithic cultures and Megalithic tombs before embarking on detailed discussion of pottery and flint types, plans of causewayed-camps and flint mines. In discussing Stonehenge it might be a good idea to relate the Wessex culture to all that has gone before and to describe continental contacts in general before discussing successive alterations

of plan and crutch-headed pins. The class will soon be asking,
"What was happening in Europe at that time?"

These two examples from British prehistory are chosen because
they are the type of problem most commonly met in classes in
Britain but many parallels could be cited from other archaeological
contexts. From this sort of deliberately over-simplified approach
many students will be willingly led on a more detailed discussion
of artifacts and specific sites.

Reference has been made to the initial capacity of some adult
students to accept archaeological reasoning. It is perhaps less
obvious that the capacity of an adult student after a day's work
is another factor constantly to be appreciated by the tutor. Most
classes take place in the evening. The tutor will be less bored with
some aspects of his subject than many of his students. He may
be less tired and certainly he is mentally stimulated during the
class session. It is rarely advisable to talk for the whole of the
class and a short but definite break about half way through the
meeting can refresh both the class and the tutor. After all, it is
normal for undergraduates to receive lectures of less than one
hour's duration at a time. Adult students are involved in considerable effort in attending classes regularly during the winter
and as many unnecessary stresses as possible should be removed
from them.

Whether or not students should be required to do written work
is one of the controversial questions in adult education. Some
form of written work is necessary in certain courses and the
perennial problem of many tutors is how to obtain it from unwilling students. Most have a horror of the idea of an "essay" and
it is sometimes necessary for the tutor to devise means of inducing
written work which avoid the necessity of writing the formal
essay. The "log-book", a digest of the previous week's class work
(lecture and discussion), prepared and read in turn by each
member of the class, is useful in many ways. Students may be
encouraged to write book reviews, to draw distribution maps and
artifacts, plans and sections.

Most students respond to the approach that they can learn only
if they are able to arrange their ideas coherently and that putting
thoughts on to paper is a useful exercise for doing this. Written
work can tell the tutor a good deal. It may be the only opportunity

he has for really personal contact with his students and may be the best guide to whether or not he has managed to present his material adequately.

Although there may be some difficulty in persuading students to write, there is little difficulty in persuading them to take a direct part in some archaeological activity. It is common, for example, for a tutor of a class in archaeology to be asked by his students whether there are any opportunities for them to take part in an archaeological excavation. Frequently a tutor has difficulty in preventing students from unsupervised digging. Reference is made below to excavation but there are other forms of active student participation.

The rôle of the amateur archaeologist has already been discussed and its continued importance underlined. A student in an archaeology class may have the opportunity of contributing directly to archaeological research, particularly that centred on his area. In this he may have the advantage of detailed topographical knowledge not possessed by the professional archaeologist who may be unfamiliar with that area. In certain favourable circumstances it is possible to combine within the scope of an extra-mural class the prosecution of archaeological research with all the essentials of good adult education. In recent years several local histories have been published based on work undertaken as part of an adult class on local history. In some cases they were written by students, in others by tutors.

Something similar may be attempted in an archaeological context but preferably covering a wider geographical area, such as a county, and perhaps restricted at any one time to a single archaeological period such as the Bronze Age, Roman Britain or Anglo-Saxon. At the present time some work on Industrial Archaeology would be particularly apposite. The greater part of the work would be systematic collection, indexing and mapping of material derived from county and national archaeological journals. In this, each member of the class taking part could hardly avoid acquiring some detailed knowledge of the particular period involved. The rôle of the tutor in such an undertaking would be that of overall director of the project. Part of each meeting would also be spent in a general discussion of the relevant material as it accumulated and the tutor would normally attempt to show its relevance to the period as a whole. Class-work would normally be associated with field-work at week-ends.

This represents a high peak in adult classes in archaeology which will probably be attained by relatively few. It is nevertheless an aim worthy of fulfilment, given the right conditions. Obviously this is not the type of project to be offered to a class meeting for the first time. An undertaking such as this would normally follow one or preferably more previous sessions of conventional type which would be important, not only for providing a sound background knowledge, but also allowing time for the members of the class to learn to know each other. Work of this kind demands close co-operation.

It must also be admitted that there are many practical difficulties, not the least in the provision of the necessary published sources. An ideal, already mentioned, is to hold the class in a library possessing the relevant books and periodicals which may be consulted not only during the class period but by students at other times. The writer's experience shows that many public librarians are most co-operative in planning a venture such as this. Relations between a county archaeological society and extramural classes can be formed and cemented through such a venture and the ideal situation, which could be achieved in many parts of Britain, would be the holding of the class in the specialised archaeological library of the local society. Whether or not the results of such a co-operative effort were published would be dependent on many factors, but the value of such an undertaking, both as an educational exercise and as a piece of research, cannot be underestimated.

Although it might be necessary for a tutor slowly to lead up to the acceptance of the idea of such a research project, there is normally little difficulty in planning an excavation. Clearly, excavation can form no part of the normal pattern of weekly meetings held during the winter, but as many excavations have been planned as a result of extra-mural classes they warrant mention in the present context.

In trying to fit excavation into the pattern of adult education, it is germane to ask how valuable and how necessary is adult student participation in a dig. It might be argued that understanding of the problems of the Iron Age or of Roman Britain may be easier for the student after working on a site of the relevant period. But how does this argument affect students in, say, the Minoan or Mycenaean cultures? It cannot, however, be claimed that excavation *per se* is vitally important to the success of an adult class in archaeology, although experience of excavation on a site of any period has a potential value in aiding the understanding of the merits and drawbacks of the technique.

Excavation as an end in itself is nevertheless valuable. If it can be associated with the type of class-work discussed in previous paragraphs, it may acquire the status of a major piece of research. Webster has shown the value of co-ordinated class-work and excavation on Romano-British sites in the West Midlands of England but this type of large-scale planning is exceptional both in its scope and its results for archaeology as a whole.[2]

Excavation is now accepted as part of the programme of Summer Schools organised by extra-mural departments and the W.E.A. In such an environment there is time to plan the excavation, techniques can be taught, equipment is available and the whole course can be formal and well organised. There is also room for similar work outside the immediate environment of the formal adult class. After a long course a tutor may have attracted small groups of interested students, perhaps drawn from several classes. If he lives in the same area as his students, a local excavation may be organised. Such excavations have taken place in recent years in several parts of Britain. The potential power for archaeological good in the existence of such well-trained groups is obvious, although being informal in their organisation their work may be hampered by lack of money. Many archaeologists believe that there is too much unnecessary excavation at present in Britain and individuals and groups are prompted to dig to satisfy some urge which has little in common with disinterested research. This tendency has in no small measure been arrested by the influence of students who have studied archaeology in adult classes.

In this chapter there has been much discussion of some of the practical problems attendant on the teaching of archaeology in adult classes. Most of these problems centre on the provision of visual aids and the relevant literature and they have been examined in the context of the traditional class which meets weekly. Some of these difficulties apply more particularly to classes other than simple introductions to the subject. They might be overcome if it were possible to experiment.

It is obvious that more advanced classes are likely to attract smaller numbers than introductory courses and an extension of the idea of the week-end school, itself now part of the tradition of adult education, might be attempted. In place of a single week-end school, a series of "linked" week-end schools, perhaps held at monthly intervals, might be attempted, each week-end consisting of three or four two-hour sessions. This experiment has been tried with success in some subjects in certain areas. In the context of archaeology classes it would have several important advantages. In large towns such a week-end school need not be residential, as it would draw on a potentially large student population, derived perhaps from several elementary classes previously held in the area. In rural areas a residential school might be preferable to enable students from a number of outlying districts to attend a conveniently situated centre. In either case the provision of visual aids and books would offer fewer administrative problems. There would be more time available for discussion and to enable tutor and students to meet informally. Such an arrangement would also help to solve the problems of supply of tutors competent to take advanced classes. Archaeologists are usually more free to travel, and to travel greater distances, at week-ends than they are during the week. Such a scheme envisages that the amount of time spent in formal tutorial work would be comparable with that of the normal weekly class of twenty or twenty-four meetings.

It must be emphasised that the views set forward in this chapter are the personal opinions of the writer drawn from his experience both as full-time and part-time tutor in several parts of Britain from suburban London to the Highlands of Scotland. They cannot claim to be definitive. Some of the particular problems of teaching archaeology to adult students, such as the provision of journals, visual aids, the necessity for class visits and the influence of the locality in which the class is held are not encountered in other subjects. The nature of archaeological material is essentially diffuse as the tutor is constantly faced with the necessity to discuss primary sources. This can be a stimulating academic discipline for students and tutor alike. In the context of general adult education archaeology should be regarded primarily as a liberal study. Most students do not wish to retain memory of the minutiae of archaeological evidence although for the purpose of class teaching much of it has to be discussed. If the student wishes to pursue his study in great depth, and many do, making of it their main leisure-time interest, he can be shown how to do so and may be encouraged to join local and national archaeological societies and to attend more specialised courses.

It means no lessening of academic standards to aim at implanting in adult students' minds the place of the prehistoric, classical and mediaeval past, as revealed by archaeology, in the whole story of man's development. In so doing, some of the techniques of archaeology will be communicated to them. They will be given the opportunity to decide individually whether or not archaeological methods and inferences are valid. They will certainly acquire an appreciation of present-day archaeological limitations. Today there is much talk of the need for popular appreciation of current advances lest scientists become the gods of the twentieth century. It is no less important to offer through adult classes present evidence as to the state of knowledge of the whole development of man and his achievements, scientific no less than cultural. If, in so doing, others are encouraged to join more actively in archaeological work in discovering and interpreting the past, then archaeology will be enriched and those archaeologists who are also tutors in adult education will receive some extra satisfaction in the fulfilment of a task adequately completed.

NOTES TO CHAPTER II

[1] cf. CORCORAN, *Adult Educ.*, **XXXII** (1959) pp. 204–11.
[2] WEBSTER, *Ibid.*, pp. 166–78.

CHAPTER III

HISTORY
AND POLITICS

H. J. Smith and
J. G. S. Shearer

HISTORY—H. J. SMITH

The common claim that history is relevant, that it is instructive for an understanding of the present, would encourage the belief that adult education provides the ideal opportunity for wide popular recognition and enjoyment of the subject. The appearance in paperbacks of a growing number of classic works of history such as those of Maitland, Coulton and Namier; or even the occasional performance by a professional historian on the television screen seem likewise to favour this expectation. The aim of adult education, that it should create for the student the possibility of informed participation in controversy and a discursive understanding of the matter under study, again suggests history to be a promising subject. Yet, in truth, when the place of history in an adult education programme is under discussion, comment soon turns to complaint about its neglect. The history of civilisations, nations and states, movements and individuals, has only a small place in the scope of adult learning. On the other hand, and perhaps by way of explanation, courses abound in subjects which appear to extract the "relevant" from history and the most recent past: international relations, politics, social and economic problems; in many others of course, the conscientious tutor does not ignore the use of a historical approach, in literature, the arts, or, say, in general courses on science.

The usual form that the study of history takes in adult education is the social history of region or county, town and village, namely local history; and similarly specialised and as locally focused is the allied study of archaeology. Neither seek to be as comprehensive as history, nor are they as ambitious of establishing large conclusions about the historical behaviour of man or of producing socially "relevant" documentation. While there are historians who deplore and question the absence of "straight" history from the adult education provision, others, more concerned with some notional purity of the subject, may feel this preserves history from the vulgarisation which they think has to be practised to make an essentially complicated subject assume shape for the layman.[1] Good local history and archaeology courses have the merit, from the latter point of view, of providing the student with an opportunity of understanding what is meant by history as a discipline, and what the historian customarily means by scientific history: practice in handling evidence and its scrupulous employment rather than the construction of systems or the discovery of laws. But apart from any question of recommendations, the study of history in adult learning appears to be divided between the two extremes of the "relevant" history of international relations and social studies; and the intricate detail and techniques of local history and archaeology. History as a whole seems to have given way before its specialised uses.

It is because they do draw on the matter of history that international relations, politics and social and economic studies can be described, for our purpose, as specialised forms of historical enquiry which have become subjects in their own right, with, of course, a marked orientation to the contemporary scene, and in this sense they make their own important contribution to the study of history. In international relations, when not taught simply as current affairs, a historical approach is naturally adopted: a course on Modern Japan in any depth will certainly take the story back to the mid-nineteenth century, and to the Meiji Restoration, a major event of history. Likewise other topics in international relations have to be introduced with something more than an artless description of antecedents. The extent to which modern pre-occupations stimulate new ways of looking at history is well known, and while strategic studies, race relations, and the problems of under-developed countries are among the more novel lines of investigation in international relations, probably they too can yield insights into earlier historical happenings. Professor Trevor-Roper can draw an interesting comparison between the triumph of Calvinism in sixteenth and seventeenth century Scotland and the triumph of Marxism in under-developed countries of the twentieth century;[2] while Messrs. Bauer and Yamey draw on Professor Southern's *Making of the Middle Ages* for a tenth century example of the servant problem in advanced economies.[3] The study of politics clearly subsumes much of British administrative and constitutional history, and that of economic and social problems necessarily touches on the historical evolution of the economy and society it describes.

Thus an attempt may be made to rationalise the absence of "straight" history from adult education programmes; the student may not consciously seek the "relevant" lessons of history but the spirit of pragmatic enquiry, even an anxious sense of civic obligation if it exists, brings him to them through international relations and the social studies; the desire for improvement, and to acquire some absorbing leisure pursuit, brings him to local history and archaeology which have a quality of fascination in common with literature and the arts. Those who regret the absence of "straight" history may possibly take some encouragement from the fact of history's diffusion throughout a number of related studies; and those who fear for the debasement of history may persuade themselves that since the subject is taught in specialised forms, the student is thereby disciplined by the particular method of inquiry which he may respect more than historical knowledge itself. The fire may be partially smothered but useful work is done in the embers.

Undoubtedly, adult education has played a notable part in stimulating and carrying forward the study of local history. The part played by television in creating public interest in archaeology is certainly better known but is not always so beneficial in result, having given rise to much careless amateur activity without expert guidance. Not a few publications in the field of local history stem from the work of tutors for their classes, and sometimes in collaboration with them. Prosaically, the rural organiser well knows the value of local history as a means of developing adult education in new centres, and of the number of long term classes it produces. Not all students in approaching the subject are desirous of becoming amateur historians despite the seeming opportunities: laudably they may be drawn by a desire to know more of the landmarks and

customs of their district: some may be moved by an irritable
curiosity about tithes and teinds, or a preoccupation with the
dissipation of local rights and the disappearance of the commons;
and in extreme cases the disappointment of a class interested only
in anecdotal and parochial trivia is not unknown. Even where
the class is favoured with the presence of the elder resident or one
grown old in the service of the parish, whose contribution of
personal knowledge is considerable, this turns out to be descriptive
rather than controversial in kind. Because the matter of local
history tends to be in the end so specialist there are some who
believe that it is not a subject in keeping with the traditions of
wide comment and discussion. The aim of a local history course
is therefore seen by some as a need, from the start, to engage the
student in the actual work of research.

If the emphasis must lie on the availability and accessibility of
evidence for direct study, then the nineteenth century is the most
fertile period. Not only is there a great abundance of first-hand
material, intelligible without difficulty to the student, exposing
all aspects of the life and work of the locality; but the nineteenth
century is also the period of most dramatic change in the place
and ways of countryside and town. It was a period of profound
economic alteration, improvement, invention and accumulation:
and of sharp deterioriation in the standards of life of the common
people; the aggravation of the problems of health, sanitation and
pauperism revealed the inadequacies of the traditional government of town and countryside, and the often brutal reforms of the
nineteenth century introduced a new age of centralised services
and professional administration. All these changes and their effects
can be studied in minute and parochial detail through the Parliamentary Papers, the printed reports and evidence of inquiries
into a wide range of subjects.[4] Only in a few capital libraries can
one hope to find a complete series of Parliamentary Papers but
local newspapers occasionally carry quite extensive and reliable
summaries of their contents where they touch on the locality.
Moreover, local newspapers from the end of the eighteenth
century, and Directories from the 1830's yield a great variety of
information accessible to the student. While the histories of
English parishes have only been carried part way forward by the
Victoria County History, Scotland is fortunate in having the *Old*

Statistical Account and the *New Statistical Account* with their
complete series of parish descriptions of the late eighteenth and
early nineteenth centuries, with a *Third Statistical Account* in
progress from 1951.[5]

With regard to particular subjects, the improvements in agricultural practice and productivity, and the remarkable spirit of
experiment that seized landlords and farmers, are shown in the
contemporary surveys of agriculture; in the form of reports to
the Board of Agriculture and prize essays; and again the Scottish
Statistical Accounts throw much light on the subject. Enclosures,
agricultural prices and wages can also be documented by reference
to newspapers and maps. The conditions of agricultural workers,
women and children included, received attention from official inquiries as in 1843, 1867 and 1893-4. The history of other forms
of economic activity, industrial, mercantile and craft, is more
irregular with its story of growth in one area and decline in
another, but here again both local and national records abound,
and in general the disappearance of the many and varied crafts
of the old community reveals one of the most important ways in
which it decayed. The impact of the economic changes of the
nineteenth century on the life and employment of the people can
be seen in intimate detail through the operation of the Poor Law,
evidence of which is probably the most prolific class of record to
be found in the English parish chest, brimming with pauper
examinations, bastardy and removal orders, together with the
occasional Overseers' Accounts. The law was amended in 1834
and its administration largely taken away from the parish, but
the printed reports of the Poor Law Commissioners thereafter
and those on health, sanitation and epidemic disease in the larger
towns continue to throw light on living conditions. For Scotland,
where the law was different, the Kirk Session Books are the chief
source on the guardianship of the poor, and the inquiry which
preceded the reform of 1845 is full of circumstantial detail for
every locality. The moral temper of the times can fruitfully be
studied through the story of religion and public education which
have their ample documentation.

One source alone which permits a vivid reconstruction of the old
community is the census. In the series of decennial censuses from
1801, those for 1841 and 1851 have survived in the form of the ori-

ginal Enumerators' Books with their entries for every member of every household in every parish. The information which that of 1851 yields on the birthplace, occupation and age of every inhabitant; the size of families; the number of domestic servants; the number of paupers; children at school and those at work; and, less reliably, the acreage of farms and the number of farm servants, is boundless in use. Further, the census of local institutions like prisons and workhouses in the parishes where they occur, add other details of value; or of the nearby "stately home" with its elaborate hierarchy of servants from Governess and Purser down to Postillion and Plate Burnisher. Also in 1851, and in separate form, an ecclesiastical census was made which reveals the extent to which Nonconformity had advanced in the English parish, and Schism in the Scottish parish.[6]

Earlier periods are probably less satisfactory for study in an adult course: there is not only less evidence with more technical problems of interpretation, but also attention is focused on topics which have become in themselves the objects of specialist historical inquiry, such as Place-names, Domesday Book, the Manor, and Church History among others. Certainly these topics can have a most absorbing interest for the student but only the very experienced tutor is capable of being more than a reporter on all of them, and only a minority of local history courses are likely to become long-term studies of the sort most fitted to do justice to such topics. There are also other themes which have their place in the history of this or that locality, yet are better studied in the context of national history: the operations of the English Civil War, the Covenanters in south-west Scotland, Parliamentary politics; even the fortunes of a prominent local family, or the career of some local worthy or priest. Local historians can make a very large contribution to the investigation of these matters but, again, for their place in national history. Naturally, and it has to be said, no tutor neglects to give his students the wider background to local history, and on the other hand, the use of local examples is one of the ways in which national history can be illumined in adult learning. Local history is not to be criticised for not being national history. It has its own strong recommendations for, indeed, the professional historian working on some detailed problem, such as the loyalties of a family in a national crisis, or the influence of regional issues on Parliamentary politics, has to become a local historian. This is true too of the social historians employing the detailed techniques of statistical analysis pioneered in France. Local history not only offers real instruction and creates a valid sense of history, but it is a subject which can clearly claim to equip the student with a new way of looking at and appreciating his environment.

The view that local history is less open to controversy and discussion than other subjects in adult education, and that therefore the choice must be of a period with the most available mass of intelligible evidence, may be contested. The experience of many worthwhile adult classes surely is that little is done in the way of research by students, and there can be no case for offering courses only to those able and willing to undertake such work. Adult education is by definition directed to working adults who are without the opportunity or leisure for becoming professional students or full-time practitioners of an intellectual hobby. With these qualifications the case for the local history of the nineteenth century is chiefly that from its many-sided and rich documentation it is possible to create a meaningful and adequate picture of the old community, its structure and life seen with greater clarity as they gave way before change and reform.

Reference has been made to international relations, the social studies, and local history, as subjects which, apart from their intrinsic merits, allow history to be taught through its specialised uses. But "relevance" to the contemporary scene or to the locality are clearly not the only tests of the value of historical knowledge. While these subjects can be numbered among the types of history, they have their limitations and they do not adequately repair the general neglect of history in the adult education programmes. The matter of international relations can conceivably permit a selection of facts which in the view of pre-twentieth century historians is distorted. Thus the Common Market and the movement for European unification have very properly received a great deal of attention: and the precedents of earlier ideas and schemes in this tradition have been recounted. It would, however, be arguable to suggest that European union is the natural issue of European history, and the facts selected may point to a historical justification of the idea but may not amount to an adequate description of previous European history. The historian of China or the Middle East in the twentieth century may indeed find the history of the political and economic transformation of industrial nations more pertinent to his theme than the story of Chinese or Arab civilisations. The historian of international relations often has to practise a dissociation of the country he discusses from its past, as well as to recommend it. He is less concerned with the continuity of the history of Africa, Asia and Middle East, than with its interruption.

Comment has already been made on local history, and again, while granting its place and function as a type of history, it is a specialist form of inquiry; its focus is specifically local or regional and not national. Specialisation is a necessary technique of teaching as well as of research, but history at large is not a syllabus of innumerable specialist topics; nor do the sectors of human life and society under study in this way have autonomy. In the provision of history in adult education it is surely important for the student to be shown the unity that exists in history of which the professional historian, working in his own field, is aware by reason of his training. History has to be seen by the student not as a circus of many turns, but as a process enabling or determining what is contained in history.

The ways in which this can be done vary. There are some epochs of history of which historians have been able to make a unified or rounded study: periods like the Elizabethan[7] or the Victorian[8] are examples of these, with their record of political and social development, of great achievements in the arts and literature, and their intellectual and scientific progress. The novelty of a society's attitudes and the ebullience of its thought and action in exploration and reform appear to give such a society a unity or even purpose which later societies do not exhibit to the same degree. A particular age in a country's history may be identified as formative, and one in which historians discover the overall historical significance of a mood as well as of enlightened or aggressive policies.

In other ways history may show that not all ages have been spent in a "bloodless struggle for office", and that alteration in human affairs has been achieved not simply by the inventiveness of bureaucrats or the innovations of managers, but also as the result of the great emancipating acts of history, whether "accidental" or "inevitable": the Reformation or the French Revolution from which so much has stemmed in the fields of religion, science, literature and the arts, as well as in the political and social development of mankind. The point is not to persuade the student of some millenarian purpose or function in history but at least to demonstrate that ultimately the specialists' history cannot replace the study of history as a whole. Moreover, the best way to help the student to appreciate the value of the specialists' explanation is to see how it contributes to the understanding of "straight" history. A means of achieving this might be by selecting periods around which controversy has sprung up, and to study the period through the controversy: the English Revolution and Civil War[9] would be one obvious choice. There is surely no danger that the student is thereby asked to make decisions rather than judgements about the history he studies, nor that he will only become acquainted with one kind of history—that of the "system-builder": for one type of historical explanation attracts another to rebut its claim and to confound it with other evidence.

The student is very ready to engage in discussion of historical controversy, about the relation of capitalism to religion, or about the place of the individual in history, or to ask the large question: Scottish students are very ready to debate the historical rights and wrongs of Presbyterianism. It would, of course, be mistaken to play to this by concocting courses which are anthologies of "big events and their interpretations". But equally the student is too ready to pass instinctive judgement on history: the venality of politicians, the futility of causes, all power corrupts and the eternal human predicament is bequeathed unsolved to the next generation. The study of history must be known to be concerned with explanation, and that historians are attempting analysis as well as description. After all, even the most eclectic of historians is, in fact, asserting that each period has its unique explanation.

A final comment should be made on the question of what is to be expected of the adult student in his approach to history. Those who argue that the subject is unavoidably devalued in the adult class fasten upon the watchword of "university standards" which is the accepted ideal of adult teaching. They fear that these standards are sacrificed to the need to communicate to a lay audience of mixed educational background. Moreover, it appears that to their minds a corollary of the ideal of "university standards" in teaching, is university attainment on the part of the student. This is not possible either, so they may argue: partly because student selection has no part in adult education, and partly because the adult student does not have the opportunity of detailed study or the access to books and necessary texts enjoyed by the student at university. This doubt about the adult student and the possibility of maintaining good standards in his instruction is not confined to the discussion of history teaching: the doubt is implicit, if not voiced, in much public and academic comment about adult education. Even within the ranks of the professional adult educationists, similar doubts are sometimes entertained, and only resolved by seeking to establish some qualitative difference between courses of lesser or greater length. Surely the doubt is founded to a large extent upon a misconception of what is actually achieved within the university: at the end of three or four years residence, the university student is not yet a historian (and it is obvious that many have no such end in view) but one who has developed a rough familiarity with, rather than precise knowledge of, the course of history, and a critical acquaintance with the various types of historical explanation rather than expertise in their application. It is not too much to hope to impart something of this to the adult student.

POLITICS—J. G. S. SHEARER

THE NATURE OF POLITICS

There is a certain ambiguity in the use of the term "politics". It may mean either a subject of academic study, like economics or sociology, which can be located with a given curricular framework; or it may mean the whole complex of questions which enter into the arena of political debate—economic growth, racial tension, defence, foreign policy, education, social justice, state aid to church schools, British entry into the European Economic Community. Indeed, there is no delimiting in advance the kind of question that may at any time form the subject-matter of political debate.

It is in this latter sense that the term "politics" is generally used and understood by the adult student. Thus the tutor in politics finds himself responding to the expectations of his students on two levels: sometimes as a "political scientist", a specialist in political theory and institutions; more often, however, as one who is expected to provide enlightenment on a whole range of practical political issues.

This has two consequences for his teaching: in the first place, he must become what someone has called a "de-specialised specialist", that is to say a specialist in his own field who is yet willing to undertake some intelligent trespassing into neighbouring academic territory; and, secondly, he must be willing, in certain circumstances, to go beyond such relative certainties as he is able to deduce from his academic studies and to enter that undefined area where different disciplines meet and where strong feelings and even passions are frequently involved. The range of his interests will thus be both far-reaching and unpredictable. Not the least of his difficulties, indeed, will be to keep abreast of the great flood of new material, and to embody in his teaching the more significant trends which it reveals.

But if politics is wide-ranging in its scope its central preoccupation is specific. Those issues are "political" which, because of their importance for society as a whole, come to be settled, either by legislative or executive action, at "governmental" level. Political debate is ultimately about the way in which the supreme civil power is exercised. It is its concern with this fundamental activity which gives to the study of politics a kind of diversity-in-unity, and it is to this general question of the use of power that the student of politics will always find himself returning.

UNDERSTANDING THE POLITICAL PROCESS

In trying to understand this complex activity the student of politics must first achieve some understanding of the total society within which political activity takes place. This is best done by enlisting the aid of certain subjects of study. The first of these is history. Since the roots of the present lie deep in the past much contemporary politics, for good or ill, will always be made up of history. Without some knowledge of the past, therefore, it is impossible to understand the present. History, studied not necessarily in detail, but in its broad outlines, should give to the student of politics some idea of the forces which have made each country what it is and of the various factors—geographical, ethnic, economic and religious—which are still relevant to its contemporary problems.

The historical approach is particularly important in considering foreign countries. Students often do not realise that other countries have their own authentic historical experiences which are no less valid for them than ours is for us. This is true, to take one example, of the United States. For a number of reasons, among them the fact that the Americans speak the same language as ourselves, there is a tendency on this side of the Atlantic to think of them simply as transplanted Britons, and then to judge them adversely when they do not behave as we do—as when, for example, we find they have no Labour Party. Because of this tendency in people to think parochially it is of the utmost importance that in dealing with the political life of countries other than his own the teacher of politics should insist that his students read as much history as possible and should himself deal with the more significant themes. Without this kind of knowledge one cannot begin to get the feel of a country's political life, or to understand its problems. There are times when, as Mr. Justice Frankfurter once said, "a page of history is worth a volume of logic".

History, then, provides the student of politics with an understanding of how things have come to be as they are. But politics is concerned not only with understanding the world, but with changing it. Accordingly, when the student of politics turns from "understanding backwards" to "living forwards" he has to turn his mind to an examination of many different (and sometimes competing) social objectives, and to settle for himself such fundamental questions as the place of man in society and in the state. Students of politics should, therefore, be encouraged to enlist the help of the great political thinkers of the past, who have provided us with brilliant insights into the human situation and into the nature of political ideas and ideals. Much of the best of that thinking has, of course, come into the ordinary language of politics and is mediated to the contemporary world through those men of ideas and political commentators who, from the side-lines, so to speak, influence the intellectual climate of opinion in which politicians live.

In view of the great complexity of most present-day political issues there are many branches of knowledge which can be made, in some degree, to contribute to the understanding of specific problems. It is not surprising, therefore, that different tutors should have different views regarding the importance, for the study of politics, of such subjects as sociology, psychology and ethics. There is, however, one subject which is of particular relevance to adult students, because it touches politics at many vital points. Whether it is a matter of economic growth in affluent societies or of rapid industrialisation in under-developed countries economic change is now a permanent concomitant of modern life. Employment opportunities, population movements, distribution of income, the class structure are all matters of fundamental political concern. The study of economics should, therefore, take its place alongside that of history and political ideas as an integral part of the study of politics for the adult student.

Lastly, there is the study of political institutions. Set within the wider historical, social and intellectual context which has been described, the study of political institutions concentrates on the actual exercise of governmental power. Each country has its own institutional machinery for bringing about political change, the product of its history and its needs. The "secret" of its constitution is never easy to understand, the spirit in which it is worked being as important as the machinery itself. It is in the field of institutions, however, that political science has achieved some of its more spectacular successes, so much so, indeed, that one recent learned report has been led to accord to political science today the same kind of status that was once accorded to theology when she was "queen of the sciences".

The student of politics, equipped with some knowledge of history, political ideas, economics and political institutions, is now in a position to work out for himself a coherent view of politics. To try to reconcile the political aspirations of his society with the political realities as he knows them is a matter requiring extremely careful and often delicate analysis. In the last resort his philosophy must be a "practical" one, in which there is no divorce between the life of thought and the life of action. "This man imagines," said Cicero on one occasion, "that he is living in the Republic of Plato, instead of in the days of that of Romulus". The student of politics must never forget that the ultimate reality, for political scientists and philosophers no less than for practising politicians, is the life of action—and that Pericles is accordingly no less important than Plato.

STANDARDS OF OBJECTIVITY

It would be plainly absurd to claim for the teaching of politics anything like the kind of neutrality that is possible in the more exact sciences. Where human feelings and aspirations are involved, the tendency within each individual mind to select what best suits its preferences and desires is inevitably a strong one. Yet this does not mean that a tutor need be unaware of his own particular "biases" or that he need do nothing about them. Indeed, he should aim at the maximum degree of objectivity of which he is capable, making every effort to present as honestly and as sympathetically as he can the views of those who disagree with him. In some cases this will require a great deal of effort, but there can be little doubt that the best tutors have always made this effort. To the extent that they have failed to do so, they have failed as tutors.

Moreover, if the word "science" is used in its French sense of "knowledge", and is not taken exclusively to mean the use of certain techniques, there is no doubt that "political science" is a perfectly meaningful term. Aristotle pointed out that every study has its own degree of certainty and that one should not ask for more. Judged by this criterion it would be generally admitted that our knowledge of the political process as a whole is steadily increasing and that this, together with similar extensions of knowledge in other fields, is making possible a more rational ordering of society. Of course, there will always be differences of opinion regarding the extent to which such "progress" is possible, much of this diversity of view deriving in the last analysis from differing views of human nature, its possibilities and limitations. Some may even find themselves adrift in Professor Oakeshott's famous ocean, where "there is neither harbour nor shelter, nor floor for anchor, neither starting point nor appointed destination". The political scientist, however, need be neither over-optimistic nor yet unduly pessimistic. He has not only reason, but a good deal of history, on his side for believing that if we cannot make of the world a Utopia, we can at least take it as it is and improve it.

"If hopes are dupes, fears may be liars."

It is certainly the responsibility of the teacher of politics to speak always with the quiet voice of reason, to appeal, in a phrase of Walter Lippmann, "to thought which is pale rather than to lusts which are strong", to uphold the view put forward by William James that reason is "a small sandbank in the midst of a hungry sea ready to wash it out of existence", yet a sandbank which is destined to grow until "bit by bit it will get dyked and break-watered". The serious study of politics hardly makes sense on any other assumption.

TOWARDS A NEW AWARENESS

There is no doubt that, as compared with the inter-war years or even the years immediately after the Second World War, political apathy in Britain is today both widespread and deep-seated. A number of recent studies of voting behaviour would seem to indicate that less than one-third of the electorate is interested in politics, that the extent of public knowledge of the issues involved is fairly limited and that in general the public cannot be said in any sense of the word to act rationally. Most people, in fact, simply judge a policy, as a Tammanay politician put it, "by what's in it for Mrs. Murphy and the kids". Even for the less unsophisticated their very familiarity with the language of politics is often mistaken for an understanding of the political process itself. Having words in one's ears, as Jeremy Bentham expressed it, is not the same thing as having ideas in one's head.

There are many possible explanations for this contemporary lack of interest in politics. For one thing, Britain's diminished rôle in the world has made her decisions seem less important, while the new centres of world power seem alarmingly remote. Again, most political problems today are extremely complicated and beyond the understanding of the ordinary man. Perhaps, too, the growing pressures towards standardisation and conformity are producing in people a kind of uncritical passivity. The chief reason, however, for contemporary political apathy is almost certainly the success with which we have achieved many of our earlier aims, a success symbolised by the advent of the affluent society. It would be a serious over-statement to say that politics has always been about poverty, but it would be hard to deny that with the onset of industrialisation it has been the existence of poverty which has presented the main political challenge. Today that challenge has been largely answered in the West.

The present state of political apathy in Britain has been favourably regarded in some quarters on the grounds that it makes political life smoother, by cushioning the circulation of successive élites. Only a small minority, it is argued, is intellectually capable of taking a sophisticated view of politics. Yet the acceptance of this view would mean, at least by implication, the abandonment of the democratic theories to which we have been traditionally committed. It would mean the end of an actively participating citizenry in the political affairs of the country.

Herein lies a special challenge to our society, and not least to those teaching politics to adults. It is a question of how far it is possible to create in adult minds a new sense of awareness regarding the whole dialogue of politics, a new realisation that political discussion *is* important. This is almost exclusively a problem for the more affluent countries of the west; in the newly evolving societies of Asia and Africa political issues make a more direct and dramatic impact on the lives of the people.

In attempting to answer this question, it is necessary to go back to the distinction made earlier between politics as a university subject and politics as an arena of debate, where fundamental issues affecting the well-being of a community come up for settlement. In the first sense it seems that there are some areas of political thought which are likely to remain minority interests. Neither political theory nor political institutions, in their academic form, are immediately attractive to the majority of adult students. The former raises difficult philosophical questions, often in a style of writing to which the student is unaccustomed, while the latter presupposes a familiarity with complex factual and legal questions. Thus, for the adult student, both political theory and political institutions tend to be acquired tastes, and to come later in his academic development. Courses provided to meet students' professional requirements, such as a course on Public Administration, designed for members of the civil service, local government and the nationalised industries, are a special case.

But of politics in its wider sense the prospects of engaging the interests of adult students are potentially more encouraging. This would seem to follow from two new factors in the situation: the advent of the affluent society, with all that this means in terms of new possibilities of personal and social enrichment; and the vast speeding-up of the rate of change, one of the consequences of the modern scientific and technological revolution.

This second factor is of particular importance in the experience of the adult student, and is thus of great concern to the adult tutor. It is true that the world has always been in a state of transition, that men have always found some difficulty in adapting themselves to an ever-changing environment, that, as Bagehot observed, "one of the greatest pains to human nature is the pain of a new idea". Yet the changing rate of change is something new in human experience. It no longer occurs so slowly that men can live their whole lives within a customary framework. Today new knowledge and new ideas come flooding in from every direction; and the adult student who wishes to take an intelligent interest in his society has often great difficulty in keeping his bearings. The problem which confronts him is a dual one: he has both to try to understand how things are actually changing and at the same time to attempt to formulate an appropriate set of values by which to assess these changes. Many of the questions which arise for the adult are questions which go beyond politics; but, since no view of social change in the contemporary world would be adequate which was not also in one of its aspects a social and political philosophy, the teacher of politics has a special contribution to make.

This means that as a result of the advent of the affluent society and the modern technological revolution a whole new range of questions falls at least partly within the field of politics in its widest sense. There are all those questions concerning the appropriate size of political communities, whether at national, international or local level; questions concerning the need for "modernisation", not only in the economic field, but in the educational field as well; questions concerning the military implications of the technological revolution—although this is a field which is becoming increasingly specialised and recondite; questions, too, which imply a revolt against mere affluence—questions of town and country planning, of amenity and taste generally; and, finally, those questions raised by the great increase in scientific knowledge and its application—touching such matters as birth control and euthanasia. These are some examples of matters that for the most part still await formulation and classification in political terms. It is on such problems as these that the intelligent citizen needs some guidance if he is not to feel bewildered and confused.

For the tutor this raises in new form the old problem of communication, of making difficult matters intelligible to an increasing number of people, without over-simplification and without falsification. It is no easy matter, as Aristotle pointed out in the *Politics*, to build a bridge between man's environment, which is complex, and his political capacity, which is simple. Yet this is precisely the kind of challenge which the adult tutor should be able to meet with a fair modicum of success. Indeed, it is the opportunities which such a challenge presents for intelligent experimentation in exposition that helps to make the teaching of politics to adults both emotionally satisfying and intellectually rewarding.

There are two temptations, however, which the tutor in politics will do well to resist. The first is the temptation to exceed his legitimate authority. Forced by the nature of his students' interests to comment on a wide variety of complex issues and accustomed to putting society and the world to rights, he will do well to remember that there are areas of knowledge which lie outside his academic competence. Likewise, he should avoid the temptation to over-rate the importance of his subject as a whole. A reasoned case can easily be made to show how politics does deeply and importantly influence our lives. But this is not to say that it is commensurate with life itself, nor that the teacher of politics is intellectually in a position to offer some all-embracing theory of the nature of social change. The days are gone when people could write of politics with the confidence of a Rousseau or a Marx or a Comte, or believe that all the ills that human flesh is heir to are remediable by political action alone. Indeed, a degree of diffidence, even of scepticism, goes hand in hand with a better understanding of the actual political process.

From the point of view of the adult student, therefore, a very wide variety of courses falls within the category of "political studies", each course having a distinctive character of its own. If there is a single underlying assumption in all such courses it is a belief in man's capacity to order his social and political life in an increasingly intelligent manner, and to bring nearer to fulfilment his often unexpressed aspirations for a society that is just, democratic and cultured. For his part, the adult tutor in politics has a useful, if modest, contribution to make.

NOTES TO CHAPTER III

[1] Some discussions of history teaching in adult classes are: W. S. ADAMS, The Discipline of History, *Adult Educ.*, **XIX**, 3 (1947), pp. 145–55; N. M. HOLLEY, History for the Adult Student, *ibid.*, **XX**, 2 (1947), pp. 87–94; N. DEES, History and the Adult Student, *ibid.*, **XXI**, 4 (1949), pp. 179–83; see also Professor E. WRIGHT, Agony and Reappraisal, *Scot. Adult Educ.*, **14** (1955), pp. 13–16. The neglect of history is reflected in its small share of the discussion of subject teaching methods in Adult Education Journals in recent years: see H. J. FYRTH and M. GOLDSMITH, Science in History—an Experiment, *Adult Educ.*, **XXXV**, 6 (1963), pp. 360–4, describing a science course in which history plays the part of an "aid".

[2] H. E. BELL and R. L. OLLARD, ed. *Historical Essays presented to D. Ogg* (London, 1963), pp. 82–3.

[3] P. T. BAUER and B. S. YAMEY, *The Economics of Under-developed Countries* (Cambridge, 1957), p. 40 note.

[4] See *Hansard's Catalogue & Breviate of Parliamentary Papers, 1000–1834* (London, 1953) and Professor and Mrs. P. FORD, *Select List of British Parliamentary Papers, 1833–99* (Oxford, 1953).

[5] The best introduction to Local History, with an excellent description of sources and profitable lines in inquiry is Dr. W. G. HOSKINS, *Local History in England* (London, 1959); very helpful also is W. E. TATE, *The Parish Chest* (London, 1952, 2nd ed.); an extensive bibliography is *English Local History Handlist* (Historical Association Special Series, S.2. 1952); see also Library Association, *The Sources of Local History* (Readers' Guide Series, 1959, 2nd ed.); for Scotland see the bibliographies of Sir A. MITCHELL and C. G. CASH, *A Contribution to the Bibliography of Scottish Topography* (Edinburgh, Scottish History Society, 1917, 2 vols.); P. HANCOCK, *A Bibliography of Works relating to Scotland, 1916–50* (Edinburgh, *1959–60*, 2 vols.); and Professor L. J. SAUNDERS, *Scottish Democracy, 1815–40* (Edinburgh, 1950), especially the references pp. 375–436.

[6] See L. C. HECTOR, The Census Returns of 1841 and 1851, *Amateur Historian*, **I** (1952–4). The 1841 and 1851 Ennumerators' Books for England are kept at the Public Record Office in London where they are available for

public inspection, and inexpensive microfilms can be obtained; those for Scotland are preserved by the Registrar General at New Register House, Edinburgh, and may be inspected on certain conditions but microfilms facilities do not exist.

[7] See Dr. A. L. ROWSE, *The England of Elizabeth* (London, 1950) and *The Expansion of Elizabethan England* (London, 1955).

[8] See Professor A. BRIGGS, *The Age of Improvement* (London, 1959).

[9] See C. HILL, Recent Interpretations of the Civil War in *Puritanism and Revolution* (London, 1958), pp. 3–31.

CHAPTER IV

ECONOMICS

Farquhar Gillanders

IN THE inter-war years adult education in Britain was much concerned with the teaching of economics, economic history and closely related subjects, with students seeking knowledge and understanding of current issues of an economic character and reaching out from personal experiences towards social and political action. In these circumstances tutors of high academic standing found it both natural and desirable to proceed educationally from the expectations and experience of their students. It was convenient, and educationally sound, to analyse in detail a current economic phenomenon, examine its development, and then seek from this standpoint an understanding of economic theory and its practical implications.

The earlier problems in the teaching of economics to mature students were not those of class-room techniques. It was accepted from the outset that it was for each tutor to work out for himself and for his class what use should be made, for example, of hand-outs, of visual diagrammatic aids, of straight lecturing, or the method of working back from present events to the underlying theory. The fundamental problem in the early teaching of economics to adults was how much theory was educationally necessary to the proper teaching of the subject. What was the proper place of pure theory in this field of adult learning? What was to be the scope of economics as a subject and what was the fundamental theoretical groundwork necessary to it as a proper academic discipline for adults?

These same questions are still, of course, live issues in all countries in the effective teaching of economics, theoretical or applied, to adult students. The evidence of tutors' syllabuses would suggest that even yet in adult education in Great Britain there is little agreement as to how the subject should be taught. The approaches to it are various and diverse; very often the syllabuses closely resemble those of internal university departments, while only too frequently economics, as taught to adults, would unfortunately appear to be more or less synonymous with sociology, politics, or even with citizenship. There is as yet no standard method of teaching economics to mature students and, surprisingly, there is not even one standard textbook on economics specially designed for their needs. One can therefore only draw on experience to suggest how the subject can effectively be taught in adult classes. And it is much easier to say how economics should not be taught to adults than to prescribe a method that will be universally applicable and acceptable.

The teaching of economics in an internal university department is very properly much concerned with theory and analysis. With adult students, meeting only for two hours once a week, it is extremely difficult even for the most gifted tutor to teach much detailed theory. The adult, one finds, continues to insist that discussion in classes must be realistic and that any worthwhile economic theory must be capable of being translated into practical politics. A mature wage- or salary-earner, on becoming a student, draws naturally on his own experience in industry, commerce, and the professions, and has an uncanny knack of questioning theory which may be held to be academically sound, but is difficult to express in terms of live issues. This salutary experience, common to all tutors of adult classes, is one from which many academic economists now tend to shrink. They find it extremely difficult to explain their theories satisfactorily even to an enlightened lay audience and, consequently, tend to insist that the theories are right and that it is the general public which is insufficiently well informed to understand them. It may be that these economists are right in their contention, but the industrialist, the administrator and the accountant seeking to put economic theory into practice often finds his hands tied in those very ways which the adult so readily forsees when pure theory is under discussion.

Adult students in a class can, and must, be taught some basic modern economic theory and tutors need not be afraid of exposing pure theory to their intelligent criticism. Theory provides the basic concepts of economics and, as such, it has to be taught. To take the easy way out and to discuss only current economic issues is to negate the purpose of adult learning. If the adult tutor takes a sustained academic line he may well lose some of his students. Yet the loss should be borne since university sponsored adult education must be prepared to insist that students study systematically such theory as is basic to a proper understanding of the subject. If the theory is then found unrealistic by the students, the tutor is immediately obliged to investigate with the class what modification may be necessary to make it applicable to everyday life. This is the substance of political economy, the basic thesis of Adam Smith's *Wealth of Nations* and of the classical economists. Increasingly it would seem, therefore, that it is political economy rather than economics that is the proper subject for study in adult education.

It is now becoming fashionable in Britain, the U.S.A. and even in the U.S.S.R., to regard political economy as a rather cruder and less well-defined study than the mathematical economics that now takes up by far the greater part of learned journals in economic science. Each aspect of the wider discipline, however, has a part to play: each is truly academic: and each is attempting to answer fundamentally different questions.

The study of economics by mature students in adult classes may well prevent the subject from becoming an obscure scholasticism, understood only by academics and senior administrators. The task of making economic theory and doctrine intelligible to a wider public is a proper social aim that the adult education movement can still properly and honourably sponsor. But it has yet to be determined how much theory is necessary for this purpose.

Professor L. G. Robbins addressing the Royal Economic Society on 7 July 1955 (reprinted in *The Economic Journal*, Vol. LXV, December 1955) discussed this central issue at some length. He was concerned with the teaching of economics not to adult students as such but to senior school pupils, to honours students at university and to those less academically committed internal students who, he argued, should not follow an honours degree course involving extreme specialisation. For a very substantial portion of university students, Professor Robbins maintained, a general degree of the kind taken under the old Scottish system and now prevalent in Canada and the United States was much to be preferred. For them he proposed a special course and his comments on its development are, it would appear, most applicable to the adult education side of economics teaching.

When we are teaching students who are not studying economics as a life study or as a profession, but who are seeking to equip themselves with an education to help them to think systematically and so to understand better the ramifications of economics and politics in the real world, then, says Professor Robbins, "we can overdo the emphasis on economic refinement". He admits that a certain basic minimum of general principles has to be taught and he argues persuasively against such a course being merely descriptive but rather that it should be concerned, as he says, with "the great elementary platitudes of the subject". The theory of supply and demand is immediately applicable but not the meta-physics of the theory of value. Descriptions of the real world he approves of as a teaching aid, as this gives students a general feeling of the background of institutions through which economic relationships develop. It is clearly important that this type of student, so easily recognised in adult classes, should know how the stock market operates and how fluctuations on the Stock Exchange quickly interact on the fortunes of firms wishing to raise capital. Professor Robbins concludes that basic theory thus applied is a more effective means of teaching such students than distinguishing with them the significance of the difference between measurable and immeasurable utility of the four kinds of cost curves.

The Robbins approach, therefore, is one most applicable to adult students; economic history is an essential complement to economics; public finance superimposed on a general understanding of the machinery of government. Generalised teaching there must be and theory and analysis must certainly be taught, but not the kind applicable to the theory paper in final honours at university.

In view of its early importance in the Adult Education movement, surprisingly little has been written on the effective teaching of economics to adult students.[1] A reason for this may be that the adult student, as a type, has changed very considerably over the years and most certainly the motives for enrolling in an economics class in the first place have possibly undergone a more fundamental change than in any other subject in adult education. The first academically organised adult education classes in economics attracted, in the main, those active men and women who were

critical of the contemporary economic order and who had shrewd
ideas as to how it could be improved. Economic theory was to
show the way to detailed investigation: and after investigation
social or political action would follow. Dr. P. Ford of the University
of Southampton argued[2] that these early students were deeply
conscious of a sense of injustice which was frequently tied up
with a particular economic theory; and it was often only the
accident of propaganda and environment that determined whether
this was land taxation, theories on social credit, socialism or communism. And Ford concluded that the first task of any tutor was
to help the student, without endeavouring to attack or undermine
his sense of injustice, to sever the analysis or theory from the
emotion. Scientific analysis, in other words, was to be applied to
economic phenomena, and economics classes properly organised
for adults did just this. They still can.

Adult students in contemporary Britain are very much less
interested in political and social action than were their earlier
counterparts. But, to a large extent, they are still deeply concerned
with the real problems, frequently of an economic nature, at the
heart of modern society: and they know that to be understood
properly these problems and stresses must be studied as an
organised discipline. Adult students of economics today, in Britain,
tend to be those few who are very much aware that the misunderstanding of fundamental issues too often lies at the root of
economic, social and political malaise. They come to economics
classes not to put the world to rights, as did the previous generation
of adult students, but rather to understand what is wrong with it.

The effective teaching of economics as a subject to adults is
related closely to social and economic change. Different countries,
at different levels of development, will find that the attraction of
economics as a subject of study will be determined primarily by
the country's particular level of industrial and social advance. In
underdeveloped countries today there is a primary interest in
economic growth: in post-war Britain there was considerable
enthusiasm for economic planning, while today's students in the
United Kingdom are more interested in the economics of wages,
inflation, the money market and international trade.

Despite this necessary variation in approach, at no time, nor
in any country, is the construction of a model syllabus a desirable

academic aim. Each individual tutor must be left responsible for his own teaching; and in the acceptance of this responsibility he is distinctively a teacher of adults. Tutors, nevertheless, most certainly can be taught how to teach more effectively and how much ground they should reasonably expect to cover in sessional or tutorial classes. This latter point is one of considerable importance for often even the syllabuses of experienced tutors in economics tend to be too embracing, too ambitious and too loose. In any course, and especially so in political economy, it is essential to begin by defining precisely what the subject is about and how and where it overlaps with other academic disciplines. Economics students must be clearly informed, at the beginning of their course, whether the subject is really scientific or whether a deductive scientific method is all that can be claimed for it.

In modern economics the academic tendency, increasingly, is towards mathematics, and away from the earlier inclination to philosophy and psychology. But having settled the method of approach to the subject, a class in economics can follow one of several well tried courses. The National Income approach is one that has been used effectively in Britain for many years and there are many standard texts using this approach that can be introduced without difficulty. An older approach and one which the writer has found even more effective is to study, in some detail, economic doctrine, not necessarily by reading the original texts, though this, of course, is very desirable, but by using such an excellent and readable book as Eric Roll's *History of Economic Thought* and thence proceeding to modern economic theory. Other tutors, however, prefer to approach economics via economic history and a three year class can usefully spend its first year acquiring an historical background, the second year in understanding economic theory and the third year in applying the theory and the historical background to the contemporary scene.[3]

With new classes the approach will, of course, vary according to the type of student that has been enrolled, but recent personal experience suggests that an approach to a first year introductory course by way of the money market and the stock exchange is one that British students now find both comprehensible and attractive. In its second year such a class could proceed easily and naturally to the theory of inflation, the concepts of National

Wealth and National Income and thence to the theories of production and distribution, concluding with an analysis of economic
organisations and institutions. Clearly, however, any course must
be adapted to the interests and the capabilities of the students,
and it is essential that the teaching should include not only the
matter and methods of the subject but also its aims. Any organised
and systematic course in economics must demand a high level of
intellectual ability and the initial enthusiasm of the student can
often only be maintained by showing that the subject, properly
treated, can be used daily to make informed judgements, and as
an aid to understanding the complexities of life in modern society.

The aim and content of an economics course having been defined,
the problem of effective teaching becomes paramount and, while
teaching at any level is an art, a consideration of techniques is a
pre-requisite to the effective exposition of the subject. At the
outset the adult tutor must be quite clear in his own mind what
it is he intends to teach, what resources are available to him and
how he can adapt himself to the class that confronts him.

A tutor of any adult class must present and prepare his subject
in an orderly sequence, but especially in the teaching of economics
he must at all times be prepared to meet and deal with prejudices,
political bias and half-digested notions about the matter under
discussion. It is his duty not only to be objective himself but to
inculcate a precision and objectivity in the minds of his students
as well. As economics is concerned with ends rather than with
means he must accept that his students, confronted with an
economic question, will naturally introduce, in discussion and in
essays, issues that are ethical, political or sociological, rather than
economic as such. An inexperienced tutor, conscious of his own
academic discipline, may tend to shy away from these side-issues,
but with more experience he will deal with them to advantage
and to the enrichment of his own learning.

In the teaching of economics it is particularly difficult to conceal
one's own political bias; the very choice of examples to illustrate
a particular theory is in itself a matter of bias. Objectivity is of
paramount importance in the sound adult teaching of economics,
though a tutor who is unwilling, if challenged, to declare his
own bias is unlikely to be very successful. The tutor must at all
times be conscious of his own bias and, as an example to his

students, he must continually and conscientiously emphasise to his class that objectivity is in itself a scholastic ideal. It is not maintained that a tutor should be timid or that he should refrain from making his own point of view known. What is asserted is that students have a right to know where the tutor stands on any specific issue; and where value-judgements on economic issues are involved it must be made absolutely clear to students that such judgements are the tutor's own. If the students in a class are always in agreement on controversial issues, it is almost certain that the teaching is defective. In an economics class, properly conducted, the students withhold judgement, do not make snap decisions and maintain a sense of proportion. It must never be the function of a tutor in such a class to teach a particular doctrine: his duty is to try to provide his students with an intellectual capacity to apply the subject objectively and systematically to particular problems that may arise.

The detailed method of teaching economics as a subject will, in large measure, determine students' reaction to it, and the tutor has to be clear, at the beginning, to what degree the subject is presented to the class for a social purpose and to what extent for the personal enrichment of the students. Professional adult tutors of economics would almost certainly regard their subject as being very much in the first category while literature, art appreciation and music, for example, they would classify as being primarily aimed at personal ends. To this extent economics tutors tend to regard their discipline as a superior one. This is an over-emphatic point of view though it is no bad thing to believe strongly in the value of the subject that one teaches. The enthusiasm of any tutor for his subject is usually infectious and more especially so, perhaps, in the social sciences.

Students should be encouraged, at all times, to write essays on specific topics that interest them as this will not only give them practice in expression but will, more than anything else, systematise their thinking in the discipline. There is no better way for a student to acquire a real knowledge of economic science than by continued written exercises in the presentation of economic facts into straightforward English. When students are persuaded to write (which is fairly easy to do), economic issues should at first be selected which call for comment and synthesis rather than for description. The ability to write is a very necessary part of adult education and a student's intellectual development will not be far advanced unless he acquires some skill in this art, and ideally each piece of written work should be discussed individually with the student concerned. It is futile to mark essays cryptically and, initially at least, they should be regarded as a private correspondence between student and tutor and should not be discussed before the whole class. As the class and the tutor integrate into a discussion group then, of course, students should be asked to read papers and this exercise, carefully arranged, can be one of the highlights of a successful course.

The initial syllabus for an economics course, sessional or tutorial, is of basic importance though it is seldom, if ever, that a good class will work its way through any syllabus prepared before the class has come into being as a social and educational unit. But the syllabus is useful, at the outset, to give the students some idea of the main ground to be covered, though it is unwise for any tutor to decide meticulously in advance how much time is to be assigned to specific topics or even in what order such issues are to be introduced. In any class, not pursuing an examinable syllabus (a rare privilege in education), the point and direction of a course will be determined generally by the discussion and the working of the group. The syllabuses of Examination Boards are straightforward academic outlines of the course to be followed: the adult class syllabus, on the other hand, is much less rigid and has two main functions to perform. It must indicate possible lines of approach to the subject in an attractive way and in its implication of standards it must be academically sound.

The syllabus is the tutor's first advertisement for his class and, as such, it requires his thought and care, and even his personality has to be brought into play when composing it. The adult tutor, more than any other teacher, has to be prepared to overstep the strict limits of academic disciplines and this, at one and the same time, is the privilege and the danger of a syllabus that is not examinable. The broad sweep of an economics syllabus for an adult class forces the tutor, no less than the student, to rethink basic issues and it permits experimentation in teaching that is denied to those preparing students for examination. But tutors in the social sciences, especially, must not profess knowledge of subjects in which they are not qualified. They must not pretend to be historians when their training has been in economics. If too much is attempted, if the syllabus is ignored too often, this will inevitably lead to a diffuse and unsatisfactory course of study and one from which students will derive little lasting benefit. A good syllabus, therefore, need not be rigid but it must be a reliable indication of what the class is going to study and it should give some guidance to potential students about reading matter.

The syllabus for an adult class in economics will be a reflection of the approach to be pursued; and an effective guide to the successful writing of such a syllabus is to trace the development that the course would normally and naturally follow were it not to be diverted into other avenues of enquiry. Three examples from successful three-year and sessional courses may be given to show natural sequence in teaching economics to adults by various methods, and from these headings a brief synopsis can be readily constructed.

THE NATIONAL INCOME APPROACH TO ECONOMICS

Definition—The various contributions to the national income—The division and distribution of the national income—Social results of the distribution—Taxation and investment—Demand and level of employment—Aspects of demand—Savings, hoarding and investment—Private and public investment—The control of investment—Excess demand—Inflation—Ineffective demand—Deflation—The trade cycle—The budget—Mobility of factors of production—Industrial organisations—Social policy—Incomes from work—Incomes from property—Wages—Profits—Distribution of profits—Social welfare.

AN INTRODUCTORY COURSE IN ECONOMICS

Definition and description of what economics tries to do—How the economy works—The price mechanism and state planning. The structure of industrial organisation—The firm, oligopoly and monopoly—The rôle of money—National income and national wealth—The joint stock company—The banks and the rôle of credit banks—Fluctuations in the economy—The trade cycle—The nature of international trade.

LABOUR ECONOMICS—AN INTRODUCTORY COURSE

(Almost every heading, here, could be developed later, with a good class, into a full sessional or tutorial class.)

The growth of Trade Unionism and the position today—Wages problems—A National Wages Policy and the National Incomes Commission—Differentials and skills—Fringe benefits—Redundancy schemes in the public and private sectors of the economy —Co-operation with management—Joint consultation and Joint Consultative Councils—Shop stewards—The strike weapon —Arbitration—The Ministry of Labour and its rôle—The rôle of the T.U.C., economic and political—The political levy and the Labour Party—Number and size of Unions—Trade Union Reorganisation—The future—Progress or Reaction?

The work of any class is sterilised unless there is an adequate supply of appropriate books available to the students throughout the course. The selection of such books for an economics class is extremely difficult and while occasionally a book appears that can be recommended to all students (e.g. Andrew Schonfield's *Britain's Economic Policy Since the War*, Penguin Special), the tutor's main responsibility is to provide a selection of representative books containing works, at different levels, in the main fields of the subject.

Students should always be actively encouraged to buy one or two books that they will always want to keep. It should, of course, be appreciated that textbooks, nowadays, are expensive and that students' resources may frequently be limited: but inculcating a respect for books is an essential part of the work of any adult tutor.

It is necessary that the books should be modern. The continuing use of books that are seriously out of date is a fault to which many tutors in economics naturally incline believing that the adult student's experience of the past should determine (and so date) the textbooks to be used. The books selected for any specific class must be determined essentially by the quality of the students. In the United Kingdom, at least, students now tend to be professional people rather than the manual workers, with which the early history of adult education is so frequently associated, and because of this a list, should not be confined to the simpler texts. In recommending books to students tutors should be highly selective and initially, at least, should prescribe chapters from a book rather than the book itself. If massive tomes are indiscriminately given to students not well versed in the use of books, despair rather than enlightenment may well be the result.

Some of the best textbooks in recent economic writing have come from the United States of America and though these tend to be very expensive to buy and, in the main, use American examples to illustrate the text, they should be freely introduced to adult students no less than to economics undergraduates at university.

Adult students come voluntarily to courses. They come, as yet, not to receive a diploma nor a degree but because they are interested in the subjects. This makes the adult tutor especially privileged in the field of contemporary education. The tutor of an economics class is even more favoured than his colleagues, for each day that passes confronts each one of us with new economic issues that are at the very heart of modern society. The subject is alive and relevant and exciting and, most certainly, it can be made interesting and stimulating to students. In 1931–32, according to a recent W.E.A. Working Party Report,[4] there were 469 classes in economics for adults in the United Kingdom (18·6 per cent of all classes): in 1938–39 the number had fallen to 200 (6·2 per cent of the classes): in 1949–50 the number had risen to 435 classes (6·8 per cent of the classes): while in 1956–57 the number had again fallen to 265 (5·1 per cent of the classes). More recent figures by the Universities Council for Adult Education do not give details for economics as a single subject, but includes it in the larger social sciences section.

An interest in economics as a subject in adult learning is, it would seem, liable to considerable fluctuations. As public interest in social problems periodically declines so will adult students tend, in the main, to become attracted to subjects that are more personal such as art and music and, to a lesser extent, literature. This is general experience in post-war Britain.

We live in a period of world tension and many people deliberately seek relief in pre-occupations far removed from the politics and economics of contemporary life. Others, however, are still deeply concerned with the problems of society and it is from this minority group that the adult education movement, in all countries, will continue to recruit its students of the social sciences. To them we have a special responsibility, and to those few amongst them who seek a knowledge of economics, but who may well be dismayed by the severity of the intellectual effort that will be demanded of them, encouragement is always appropriate. Economics is concerned, primarily, with the betterment of human life. In isolation, economic theory is arid and unexciting but related intelligently and purposefully to the pressing problems of our time it can inspire both confidence and hope. There is no easy road to a sound knowledge of economics and, as an academic discipline, it will always be a difficult task for the adult student to subject its theory and doctrine to systematised study. Properly understood and wisely used economics can, however, reduce the frictions due to conflicts of interest that now exist between man and man, between groups and between nations. Its future contribution to the welfare of mankind may be decisive.

Economics deals with matters which men find very close to their lives. It is a subject of study that will always attract the serious adult student.

NOTES TO CHAPTER IV

[1] The following articles, pamphlets and books are particularly recommended to potential tutors and students. Some of these have very particular relevance to the teaching of economics to adult students; others are of more general interest.

British Institute of Adult Education, Report of Proceedings at First Conference—Oxford—1922. Section on the teaching of Economics.

G. D. H. COLE	The Teaching of Economic History and Theory, *J. Adult Educ.*, **I,** 2 (March, 1927).
P. FORD	Some Problems in the Teaching of Economics, *Adult Educ.*, **VII,** 1 (Sept., 1935).
R. CANT	The Teaching of Economics, *Adult Educ.*, **XXIII** (Sept., 1950).
A. JOHNSTONE	*Some Problems Associated with the Teaching of Economics* (Central Joint Advisory Committee on Tutorial Classes, 1950).
G. D. BARKER (ed.)	*Economic Education Journal of Educational Sociology* (March, 1950).

L. SILBERMAN	Economics on the Job. *Further Educ.*, **III**, 4 (May, 1950), on the teaching of economic theory in relation to a particular industry (aluminium).
	The Teaching of Social Science in the United Kingdom (U.N.E.S.C.O., 1954).
	The Social Sciences in Secondary Schools. Reports and Paper on Sciences, 4 (U.N.E.S.C.O., 1955).
L. ROBBINS	The Teaching of Economics in Schools and Universities, *Econ. J.*, **LXV** (December, 1955).
A. M. CARR-SAUNDERS	The Place of Economics and Allied Subjects in the Curriculum, *Econ. J.*, **LXVIII** (Sept., 1958).
A. B. CHEYNEY	*Educating Teachers in Economics* (Ohio Schools, Oct., 1958).

Economics Association, *The Teaching of Economics* (1961).

E. HORN (ed.) *Methods of Instruction in the Social Sciences* (Scribners, New York, 1937).

[2] P. FORD, *op. cit.*, p. 3.

[3] L. ROBBINS, *op. cit.*, p. 587 passim. (A description of how economics could be approached by university students reading for a general degree as opposed to an honours degree;

[4] *Aspects of Adult Education.* Working Party Report, p. 38 (W.E.A., 1960).

CHAPTER V

AN ASPECT OF INTERNATIONAL RELATIONS:

ASIAN STUDIES

R. A. Williams

Without knowing . . . some people other than ourselves, we remain, to the hour of our death, with our intellects only half expanded; we cannot divest ourselves of preconceived notions. There is no means of eliminating their influence but by frequently using the differently coloured glasses of other people, and those of other nations, as the most different, are the best. (John Stuart Mill.)

IS THERE AN AUDIENCE FOR ASIAN STUDIES?

Any discussion of adult interest in Asian studies has to recognise that the articulate demand for such courses is not great. As the report of the working party on "Asian Studies in Adult Education" puts it: "The point was constantly made that it was not so much that people were positively uninterested in Asian affairs as that they did not articulate a demand for appropriate courses. Since there was also an acute shortage of tutors qualified to deal with Asian problems, this meant that providing bodies had no incentive to include Asian studies in their prospectuses".[1]

If, however, such courses are provided, experience suggests that there would be no lack of response. Faced with manifold crises, confused political situations, and a rapidly changing Asian scene, it would be surprising if this were not so. Today, Asia is constantly in the news, Asians are increasingly becoming visitors to our cities both as students and as immigrants, and there is a growing awareness of our general ignorance of Asian countries and cultures.

Though the latent interest in Asia exists, it has also to be admitted that the overwhelming majority of adults have little or no previous background knowledge of Asia, whether of its countries, cultures, or peoples: scant attention being paid to any aspect of this continent in our schools and all too little in our universities.

Accordingly, adult students are likely to attend courses on Asia from motives of curiosity, from a desire to learn something of peoples of different backgrounds and cultures, from a wish to understand current happenings more fully, or because they realise their ignorance of almost half the human race. But usually they will have no firm ideas as to what specific content should be included in such courses. All too often this will be left to the judgement of the tutor.

How, then, can the students' interest be capitalised, developed, and satisfied? How, in fact, can the subject be taught? What are the appropriate methods? How should the content of the course be selected?

What follows is an attempt to answer these questions and to indicate one possible approach to the adult teaching of Asian studies.

TEACHING METHOD

From what has been said already, it would seem to follow that, initially at least, exposition on the part of the tutor will perhaps play a greater rôle in the presentation of the subject-matter than in many other fields of liberal studies. Without prior knowledge of what Hinduism involves, its implications can hardly be discussed. Without a grasp of either the geography or history of China, a discussion of the influence of geography on China's development is out of the question.

The tutor must of necessity devote a good deal of time to exposition, but this should neither be overstressed nor should it be taken to mean that discussion is ruled out altogether. However, it does mean that such discussion will have to be carefully handled to ensure its pertinence. For example, the balance-sheet of the advantages and disadvantages of Communist rule in China can only be discussed at the end of a course on Modern China, not at its commencement.

Admittedly, if the course is mainly concerned with Modern Asia, student comment will be more plentiful. Topics such as population pressure, under-developed economies, the growth of nationalism, present-day leading Asian political personalities, all readily lend themselves to discussion because they are all to some extent within the students' frame of reference. But if the course is more closely concerned with examining the political and cultural background and development of Asia, or of a particular Asian country, then such wide themes for discussion do not so obviously or immediately present themselves.

However, should the tutor therefore conclude that the only remedy is for him to lecture for the whole two hours of the meeting, any latent interest in Asia is soon going to evaporate.

Even in considering those aspects of Asia's past that do not readily lend themselves to discussion, the discussion period can be still profitably used:

(i)   to allow questions and comments from class-members;
(ii)   to enable the tutor to ask his audience questions in order to seek out any misunderstandings;
(iii) for re-capitulation;
(iv)   to serve the same function as foot-notes do in a book, i.e. to expand on certain themes, to introduce new detail.

In any event, it will soon become obvious as the course develops that Asians have faced and tried to answer all the basic problems that have confronted mankind generally: problems such as the meaning of life and death, the relations between man and man and between man and the State, and how to organise the good society. Once this point is reached—and many Asian peoples reached it very early in their histories—and once it is appreciated that the Asian attempt to solve these problems is often along very different lines from those in the West, then a wealth of discussion is likely to ensue. It is at this stage, when some students may reconsider their basic beliefs in the light of these differences, that John Stuart Mill's quotation is particularly apposite. Mill was actually pleading for the study of the humanities, but what he says is also very applicable to the study of China or India; while Max Muller once wrote: "If I were to ask myself from what literature we here in Europe, who have been nurtured almost exclusively on the thoughts of the Greeks and Romans, and one Semitic race, the Jewish, may draw that corrective which is most wanted in order to make our inner life more perfect, more universal—in fact, more human, I would point to India."

Naturally, in order to maintain student interest and to facilitate teaching, the tutor will employ all the well-tried adult education techniques of using maps (a necessity for Asian studies) and, where appropriate, visual aids.[2] He will also perhaps find it an advantage to split up his talk into two, or even three, 20 to 25 minute "sprints" rather than just give one marathon delivery. Not only is the attention of adults more easily held in this way, but most of them seem to prefer it. Moreover, by dealing with the various aspects of a topic separately whenever possible, it tends to make the discussion more relevant by encouraging pertinent discussion of limited issues. What tutor, at the end of an hour's talk, has not found the questions and comments all too often centring upon only the last two or three points that he raised?

Perhaps the prime requirement, though, in order to aid adult learning is the simple one of a blackboard and chalk. Names of Asian places and people and technical terms, should always be written on the board and left there for the duration of the meeting so that students can make constant reference to them. This, especially if the main headings of the talk itself are also written down, is another aid to discussion.

Adults seem to find most difficulty with the pronunciation of Asian names. Bearing in mind the length of some Indian names and the multiplicity of the Chinese Changs, Chengs, Chungs and Chings, this is not surprising. Even writing them on the board is not going to be of much assistance if the tutor then proceeds to give them their correct pronunciation. This way lies utter confusion—your written "Ch'ên" becomes your spoken "Chun" your written "Sama" your spoken "Summer". So, with some hesitancy and doubtless to the horror of the language specialist, the writer would suggest that Asian names be pronounced as they would if they were English. For some important names one would obviously want to give the correct pronunciation, but otherwise this method does lead to greater clarity and is less distracting to the average adult. Though, naturally, the tutor would have to inform his class at the outset if he intends adopting this procedure.

Even the employment of all the above-mentioned teaching methods will fail to maintain the students' interest, if the tutor fails to bring out the significance of what he is saying in the clearest and most interesting manner possible. As the question of lecture-presentation is here inextricably interwoven with the question of lecture-content, perhaps this point can more properly be discussed in a later section.

READING AND WRITTEN WORK

As we have seen, the necessity for exposition in communicating Asian studies to adults by no means precludes their participation in discussion. Nor does it mean that they should play an inactive rôle in furthering their studies. Wide reading and some written work are indispensable. While this is no doubt true of any subject, it applies with perhaps even greater force to a subject where most students start from scratch, with no previous acquaintance with the terms or the ideas of the culture concerned.

Only by wide reading can student progress and interest be maintained. Once such reading is undertaken, not only is the tutor's task correspondingly eased, but the student may find himself embarked on a lifetime's reading about various aspects of China, India, Japan, or whichever Asian country it may be.

It is therefore vital for the true success of any course that there should be an adequate and imaginatively chosen class library and that the tutor should actively encourage his students to read the books available. It is useless merely to refer students to a public library; most of the books mentioned during the course should be in the class library. Some academics may think that this encourages student laziness or may argue that if the students are really serious they will get hold of the books for themselves. A few may indeed do so from the very commencement of the class, but *after* their interest has been aroused in the books available in the class library, many more will do so later. Anything that makes it easier to obtain books should be encouraged.

This is particularly so because reading plays an integral rôle in the success of a class. Once a student's enthusiasm has been caught by his reading, it is much easier for the tutor to maintain his interest in the subject. Reading instils fresh life into the framework of the study as provided by the tutor's lectures. Conversely, the tutor can help to bring out the significance of the books and so aid the students' enjoyment and understanding of them.

Great care, however, must be taken in the selection and distribution of the books. A class library should not be confined to a few accepted standard works, otherwise some students will attempt to read them, find the going too hard, and give up hoping to read round the subject at all. Whereas, if the books had been more imaginatively chosen and if the student had been advised as to what to read and the order in which to do it, this catastrophe —for such it is—could have been avoided.

A class library for Asian studies, just as those for international relations and history, should contain biographies, autobiographies, and novels, as well as well-written works on history, politics, sociology, and art. A rich vein is waiting to be tapped here.

There is no shortage of books suitable for adults in the field of Asian studies. Readable, interesting, and profound historians like Fitzgerald and Goodrich in the case of China, or Spear and Basham in the case of India, can be approached via the literary translations of Arthur Waley, *The Good Earth* of Pearl Buck, or even via the detective stories of van Gulik, while many contemporary and older novels have something valid to say about the Indian scene and mind. Indeed, the poet, artist, or novelist often afford the deepest insight into any particular country, and it would be criminal not to increase the students' understanding and enjoyment of the country concerned by failing to use their services.[3]

There is, perhaps, no greater reward for a tutor than to see his students reading avidly.

As for written work, the writer would prefer to see his students reading widely than writing badly. Though one convenient way of killing the two birds with the one stone is to encourage the writing of critical reviews of the books they read. This is a valuable discipline and one that makes for serious reading, as well as giving the tutor some idea of the progress the student is making. Moreover, all students should be encouraged to take short notes of the lecture material and to jot down any point that they may wish to raise later in the discussion.

CONTENT

How should the topics for a course on Asian studies be selected? Where do adult interests lie? How can such a course best satisfy their needs whilst still providing a systematic and disciplined study? Here, attention will be paid less to sessional or shorter courses than to one possible comprehensive course designed to give adults a basic introduction to Chinese or Indian studies. Some of the comments might also be found applicable to any regional approach to international relations or to African studies.

Sessional or shorter courses are, by their very nature, almost bound to confine their scope to limited topics. Otherwise, if an attempt were made to cover the whole of present-day Asia in a sessional course, the focus would probably have to be concentrated on the three dominating themes of Poverty, Nationalism, and Communism. In any event, little time could be devoted to the cultural heritage of individual Asian countries, and their histories could only be delineated. In itself, this could lead to grave misunderstanding of the present, while it is also doubtful if, after completing such a course, the class-members could readily distinguish between nationalism in Burma from that in, say, Malaya. Experience suggests that it is the similarities rather than the diversities that will be remembered, that Asian nationalism, for instance, will tend to be seen as a simple strand rather than as a complex and tangled skein.

But in view of what was said earlier, the biggest draw-back to short courses is that they do not allow the students sufficient time to develop their interest in, to read around, and to understand fully, a particular subject.

Consequently, it can be suggested that it is preferable to pursue a national study, though Chinese, Indian, or Arabic studies would better qualify for the term "regional study", over an extended period. A three-year period seems to be of ideal length, though no obligation to attend for three years should be demanded of a student. The tutor should accept the challenge of maintaining the interest of the majority of his students over the three years, so that they would wish to return each session. In this way the student's need for time in which to come to grips with the subject can be provided.

That a "study in depth" is advocated might be thought to clash with the normal adult desire for variety and spice in his studies, and to be too restricted in its appeal. In fact, though, the two can be legitimately blended, and such a course can provide systematic study as well as satisfying the adult's demand for variety.

Superficiality should have no place in adult education: for it is in extra-mural work that a stand should be taken against the pressures toward the superficial treatment of serious subjects which are fostered by many of the mass media in contemporary society. But this does not mean that adults have to adhere to a rigid syllabus: they can quite properly and profitably rove the by-ways as well as the high-ways of a subject. While the very nature of the civilisations of China and India allows a blend of both systematic study and linked variety.

Both India and China possessed a well-knit, unified culture such as Europe has not known since the Middle Ages. Every aspect helps to illustrate other aspects, each is of value in the study of the others. To understand Chinese painting fully, for example, one would have to be acquainted with the history, myths, philosophies, and religions of the country, while the recent exhibition of Indian arts at the Edinburgh Festival brilliantly showed how closely interwoven are Indian music, dancing, art and sculpture. The guide-book to this exhibition quotes the story of a king once asking a great sage to teach him how to make sculptures of the gods. The sage replied: "Someone who does not know the laws of painting can never understand the laws of sculpture." "Then," said the King, "be so kind as to teach me the laws of painting." The sage said: "It is difficult to understand the laws of painting without understanding the technique of dancing." "Please then instruct me in the art of dancing." "This is difficult to understand without a thorough knowledge of the principles of instrumental music." "Please teach me the principles of instrumental music." "But," said the sage, "these cannot be learned without a deep understanding of the art of vocal music." The king bowed in acceptance. "If vocal music is the source and goal of all the arts, please then reveal to me the laws of vocal music."

Since the nature of their cultures are so closely integrated, references to Chinese novels, painting, poetry, and theatre, can serve to illustrate the political and social life of the country, as well as being of great interest in their own right. Similarly, reference to the Indian arts can illumine the Indian social and religious scene. Indeed, it is only by some exploration of the poetry and arts, the beliefs and values, of any particular Asian country that we can hope to form a balanced appreciation of its culture. The very variety, provided it is not overdone, helps to show the essential unity of these cultures, and in no way hinders systematic study.

So, what in fact should a three-year course on, say, China cover? While this will depend on the particular interests of the class and tutor, one suggestion would be:

1st year: A survey of the origins and flowering of Chinese civilisation to 1289 and the advent of the Mongols. Among topics, other than the political and social evolution of the country, to which some reference could be made are T'ang dynasty poetry, Han dynasty, and earlier, bronzes, cave temples, early developments in Chinese science, the scope of Chinese philosophy, etc.

2nd year: The decline of Chinese civilisation and the impact of the West, particularly in the nineteenth century. Reference could be made to Chinese drama, novels, porcelain and painting.

3rd year: The China of Chiang Kai-shek and Mao Tse-tung.

Such a course could be initially advertised, under the title, "Chinese Studies: The Ancient Civilisation of China", in the following manner:

This was a civilisation quite different from any other the world has ever known, as well as being the world's oldest continuing civilisation. A study of its social, political, and cultural history, besides being of unusual interest in itself, is essential if Modern China is to be fully appreciated. Mao Tse-tung, it might be said, can only be fully known if one knows Confucius.

China's politics, art, culture, and religion were closely interbound, so that a study of a Chinese painting, of the life of a Chinese poet or philosopher, will tell us much about Chinese political life and the Chinese mind. Conversely, unless we understand the social and political background out of which it arose, no appreciation of Chinese art is possible. Accordingly, an attempt will be made to trace not only China's political and social history, but also her cultural development.

During the first year, China's pre- and early history will be considered, but, should there be a demand, the course will be continued in subsequent years to take the story of China down to the present time. It is stressed that anyone interested in Modern China will gain a deeper understanding by studying the ancient roots from which it grew.

The form of this entry has relevance to what was discussed in the opening section. The potential audience for Asian studies can broadly be divided into those who have some interest in the subject but who have no definite ideas as to what to expect:

these, obviously, present no problem. On the other hand, there are those who are more particularly interested in current Asian political events. Here there is a very real problem.

While it is a myth to believe that adults are interested only in current Asian affairs, many do want to be assured that a study of Asian history is of relevance to an understanding of the present. Fortunately, this assurance can be readily given. To appreciate the rôle of Mahatma Gandhi, a knowledge of Hinduism and of the Bhagavad Gita would seem essential. Without a study of the caste-system it is difficult to realise that tackling the problem of India's rural poverty is no simple matter of economics. Without an attempt to assess Communist China in relation to the country's traditional institutions and traditional pattern of thought, we can hardly hope to see it in perspective and will tend to view it solely in terms of our own Western background and experience. Whereas a study of China's history will reveal, among other things, that many features of Communist society—the centralised, élitist government, the subordinate rôle of the individual, the orthodox doctrine applicable to all aspects of life, the rôle of the bureaucracy —are by no means foreign to the Chinese scene.

Accordingly, as was mentioned above, the tutor must try to bring out the significance of what he is discussing at every step. In this, the very nature of the subject matter assists him: the Confucian view of poetry can be compared whit that of the Marxists, the Literary Inquisition of Ch'ien Lung with the "thought control" measures of the Chinese communists, Yuan Mei to Hu Feng, in addition to the much deeper sesne in which Asian history is essential to an understanding of the present.

Because some adults seem more interested in current events, tutors might feel inclined to embark on the course suggested above in the reverse order. The present tutor's experience has been that if one begins with the history of the first and second years, then, in the third year those who are not politically inclined and who would not originally have attended such a course, have still a sustained interest and are, to their surprise, enjoying the "politics". Whereas it is very much more difficult to persuade the politically-inclined to go back into the history after covering the modern period.

To the writer, the most interesting and perhaps the most important aspect of the modern age has been the impact of

Western civilisation—at base, the export of the Industrial Revolution—on the older civilisations of Asia, and the resulting revolutionary developments that have ensued. Even so, he would not wish to suggest that courses on Asia should begin with the story of the Western impact. Unfortunately, the civilisations of both China and India were then in a periodic "trough", and it is most regrettable that, for most of us, the history of India begins only with Clive, and that of China with the Opium War.

It seems very important that any course on Asian studies, whether on Modern Asia as a whole or on Modern China or India separately, whether it deals with the rise of Asian nationalism or the problem of Asian economic under-development, should devote at least some of the opening lectures to tracing the earlier achievements of these civilisation and the debt—all too often unacknowledged—that our Western civilisation owes to them.[4] The sooner the interdependence of the evolution of the world's culture is more widely appreciated, the better for all. Then one might genuinely hope for a reduction of prejudice and of international tension.

SUMMARY

What can the adult hope to achieve by attending courses on Asian studies? First, enjoyment: it would be an unusual student who could not find something of interest and enrichment in the vast field of Asian literature or art, or from the sweep and range of its history. Second, understanding: both of other people and their beliefs, and of ourselves. Third, a mind made both more tolerant (toleration being the prime traditional Asian virtue) and more critical.

The tutor's satisfaction comes from successfully stimulating his students' interest in this most important and fascinating subject.

NOTES TO CHAPTER V

[1] *Final Report on the Conference on Asian Studies* held at Liverpool, 13–16 July 1962, under the auspices of the United Kingdom National Commission for U.N.E.S.C.O.

[2] It is often said that there are a great lack of visual aids on Asia in this country. Though this is undoubtedly true, many books on Asian Art, archaeology and geography do provide useful visual material, while, in the case of China, a small subscription to *China Reconstructs* can build up a useful collection of such aids within the space of a few years. *China Reconstructs* is a glossy,

highly-subsidised, communist propaganda monthly magazine, whose articles—except those on archaeology, which are often useful—are heavily biased, but it does publish excellent photographs of the China scene and of various aspects of Chinese art, architecture and archaeology.

[3] In the case of India, the obvious literary works of Tagore, Kipling, and Forster can be supplemented by contemporary novelists such as, R. K. Narayan, Mulk Raj Anand and R. Prawer Jhabvala. See: G. M. CARSTAIRS, *The Twice-Born* (Hogarth Press), an appendix to which contains an imaginative list of books for further study, as does Hugh Tinker's *India and Pakistan* (Pall Mall).

[4] See: J. NEEDHAM, *Science and Civilisation in China* (Cambridge University Press).

L. C. GOODRICH, *A Short History of the Chinese People.*

A. L. BASHAM, *The Wonder that was India* (Sidgewick & Jackson).

G. T. GARRATT, *The Legacy of India* (Oxford University Press).

R. DAWSON, *The Legacy of China* (Oxford University Press).

CHAPTER VI

FOREIGN LANGUAGES

C. J. Titmus

IN DISCUSSING the value and function of any subject of adult learning, the writer may begin with two questions. What has the subject by its own nature to offer? What does the adult seek to gain from his study of the subject? That one will not always receive the same answer to these two questions is perhaps a truism of adult education, but since the truism points to one of the adult tutor's continuing dilemmas, it requires to be stated. Should he try to reconcile what the subject can properly give with what the student wants, or perhaps lead the student to accept what the class can provide, although it may not correspond with what he came to seek? How far should the tutor go in either of these courses? Is he justified in adopting a "take it or leave it" attitude, confident in the belief that he is doing what can and should be done in his subject, taking no account of the wishes and circumstances of the students?

First of all, let us try to answer the two basic questions in the context of foreign languages. A language is primarily a tool. It provides a means of communication between human beings, or, in the case of those artists such as Kafka, more interested in formulating their own problems than in presenting them to other people, a means of self-expression. A language class will therefore offer the student mastery of a technique. It will become as much a practical study as needlework, woodwork or pottery. In everyday situations it may enable the student to speak and to understand the speech of others, to write and read. It is a technique for successful living with the native speakers of the language.

On another level it opens the way to appreciation of a foreign culture through its literature (here taken in its widest sense to include newspapers, magazines and other ephemera). Indeed, many would say, with some justification, that literature can only be truly experienced in the original language.

Few will cavil at the claims made for the value of learning a foreign language as an instrument. Other claims, however, may appear more doubtful. It is not uncommon for teachers to maintain that language learning confers some benefit by the extent and kind of intellectual effort it requires.[1] This may indeed be a valuable by-product of learning a foreign language, as of a number of other subjects, but it could not by itself justify the inclusion of foreign languages in the adult curriculum.

One other claim will stand closer scrutiny. Languages evolve to give expression to man's thought. What man thinks and wishes to communicate is conditioned by the social and economic circumstances under which he lives, as well as by the basic and eternal pre-occupations of human nature. Therefore, language, reflects to some degree the society of the people who use it. Since modern languages have changed less over the past few hundred years than the societies which use them, they reflect also the past history of these societies. Not only that, abstract thought is only possible through the medium of language, therefore each individual is influenced and limited in his thinking and his communication by the language he uses. Different languages express the same objective facts by different concepts. As a simple example, the time 7.30 is "halb acht" in German, but "sept heures et demie" in French and "half-past seven" in English. The German conceives of this time as part of the eighth hour, but to the French or English speaker it is part of the seventh.

Different peoples are therefore conditioned in their habits of thought, in the way in which they react subjectively to objective facts, by their native language. It is one way, and not the least profound, in which their society and its history affects them. Learning a foreign language may teach the student that such differences exist. It may make him more aware of the social importance of language, of the problems of human communication and of the difficulties of understanding between peoples.

The motives that draw adults to undertake voluntary study of any subject are of daunting complexity. Not only do they vary widely from individual to individual, but one person may be fired by a number of motives. What is more, it is often extremely difficult to assess the true reasons which draw the student and to know what he seeks. This is because of the subjectivity of any response to the question, "Why do you come to the class?" There is much evidence to suggest that the majority of students have no clear idea of their reasons for taking up a subject. They decide that they would like to study history or literature; they do not examine their own motives until the questions of a tutor or a friend force them to do so. Some are then honest and admit they do not know, or are unable to formulate their reasons. Others, not necessarily less honest, since the process is not conscious, rationalise their action in attending the class and attribute to it a motive that is plausible and academically respectable, but which may not be the true one.

In foreign languages the situation is complicated by the dual nature of the subject, both practical and cultural, technique and content. Many adults study a foreign language for vocational reasons. Their motives are clear and the tutor can assume that they will be willing to work hard outside the class. They and the tutor have an equally clear idea of what they seek in the course. However, their special interests make it difficult, not only to meet the two kinds of vocational demand in one class, but even more to satisfy them in the same class as non-vocational students. Professional language examinations, like all academic examinations, lay principal emphasis on the written language, on the academic and, for most people, practically useless exercise of translation into and out of the foreign language. The curriculum for such students must approximate closely to that which schools are forced to adopt for their examination candidates, in which oral fluency and an ability to understand the spoken tongue are of minor consideration.

The business man has no such academic formalities imposed upon him. He needs to speak and write, to understand the spoken and written language. His demands on the class time are thus incompatible with those of the examinee. They are also difficult to satisfy in the same class with non-vocational students. The strength and urgency of his motive, the time he will devote to the subject mean that the tutor must set a pace that the adult with a weaker drive cannot achieve. Furthermore, the student who needs a language for business reasons will commonly need a specialised vocabulary, in addition to his general one. It may often be a waste of time for the non-vocational student to learn this.

Outside those with an immediate vocational use for a foreign language, there are others, commonly included in the non-vocational group, who nevertheless take up a language with some specific, perhaps semi-vocational use of it in mind. The man, who, although having no urgent requirement, believes that a foreign language may be a business or professional asset at some time: the professional linguist who wishes to add another language to those he already knows: the person who intends to spend a holiday abroad: who desires acquaintance with a foreign literature and rightly believes it can only truly be appreciated in the original. Their motives are not normally so strong as those of the first group, but they are clear enough and it is fairly simple to see what they seek from study.

Then there is the third category, which has in mind no clear application of the subject. It includes those who take up a language for its own sake, as an academic discipline, who study it not as a means, as a tool to be mastered, but as an end, for the interest and satisfaction they find in its structure and its formal patterns, for the light it casts on the modes of thought of the men who have developed and use it. This group may, of course, and often does comprehend the professional linguist.

Also in the third category come those whose interest is neither practical nor academic. There are those who say, "I have forgotten nearly all the French I learnt at school. It seemed such a waste, so I thought I would brush it up." This alleged motive probably conceals in many cases what may be called social or psychological reasons. People come to classes for the companionship they find there, often because a friend or neighbour is also a member. Others find in adult education the satisfaction of sharing in meaningful activity which they do not experience outside the classroom. There is order and coherence which provide a refuge or a solace for the incoherence of existence. What other explanations account for the return of some people year after year to the same elementary class, apparently making no progress, but quite content? For what other reasons do so many students ask to undertake the old grammar grind they underwent at school and which conspicuously failed for the most part to give them any practical command of the language?

No doubt many of the students who can give no motive for their
enrolment in the class seek some sort of therapeutic value from
language learning. But not all. In recent years to have a smattering
of a foreign language has acquired a snob value, just as holidays
abroad have. As touring overseas has become more common,
however, mere travel has lost its cachet. He or she who wishes to
shine must show a knowledge of and a taste for foreign dishes and,
equally, demonstrate an acquaintance with foreign tongues.[2]

This certainly incomplete survey of motives and aims will
suggest a further complicating factor for the planner and teacher
of adult foreign language classes. Adult students vary widely not
only in why they come and what they desire, but in how deeply
they desire it. Upon the strength of their incentive will depend to
a large extent what the tutor and they may hope to achieve. In
general, the snob and the student who comes for social or psychological reasons will be more easily discouraged than the semi-
vocational one, and none of them will be prepared to make as
great an intellectual effort as someone with a compelling vocational
need of a foreign language.

Of course the student's native ability is a prime factor in limiting
what may be done. So, too, tutors would agree, is his previous
educational experience. The tutor is considerably assisted if the
student is trying to recover a forgotten skill, however imperfect
it may have been at its best, and probably more so, if the adult,
taking up a new language, already has a good grasp of a foreign
tongue. The absolute beginner, with no previous experience of a
second language, presents a far more difficult challenge.

In large centres of population, where a number of parallel
courses are offered in a single language, it is possible to reduce
the complexity of the tutor's task. Classes may be advertised to
appeal to different interests and levels of experience. There will
be classes for public examination candidates, specialised vocational
courses, such as Russian for scientists, classes for non-vocational
beginners having previous knowledge of language learning and
classes for absolute beginners. Since demand in adult education
can never be exactly predicted, it is advisable not to advertise all
the classes for a fixed public, but to suit the emphasis of the
course to the demand revealed by enrolments. Some form of
selection, or at least of counselling, carried out before the beginning

of the session, will assist students to find the class best suited to their needs and talents.

There is little doubt that the homogeneous classes achieved by this kind of selection will lead to greater teaching efficiency, and that with the growing demand by adults for foreign language classes, selection will be easier. At the University of Glasgow in 1962–63, one first-year evening class in French attracted 154 enrolments. In other languages there was an even greater demand and it was found necessary to arrange 5 first-year classes in French, 8 in Italian, 8 in German, 4 in Spanish and 3 in Russian. More could have been offered had there been sufficient tutors.

Selection certainly imposes an added burden on a usually inadequate administrative staff, but the main objection to it is one of principle. Traditionally, the non-vocational adult class serves a social purpose, by bringing together people of diverse social, professional and educational backgrounds in a corporate activity. It is an exercise in democratic living, made possible because it draws an undifferentiated public. Any form of selection is incompatible with this aim.

Valid though the aim may be, it can only be achieved if the student continues to attend the class. All experience shows that the student wastage rate for non-vocational foreign language classes drawing upon an undifferentiated public is high. In 1962–63 classes in 15 modern languages were offered within the precincts of the University of Glasgow. For these 1903 people enrolled, but only 981, or 51·5 per cent, completed the session. In beginners' classes the situation was rather worse, only 43·5 per cent of those enrolled continued to the end. These figures are not exceptional, they merely confirm the evidence of tutors in other centres.

Very little accurate information is available about the reasons for student wastage.[3] It is, after all, difficult to question people who are no longer there to be questioned. Some will find it impossible to attend the class any longer, but the proportion so affected will be no higher than in any other subject. The others, probably the majority, abandon their studies because of some dissatisfaction, the cause of which they would be hard put to it to explain. Most, however, may be presumed to give up because they do not find in the course what they seek, either because of personal inadequacy, or because the course does not offer it.

The tutor's solution would seem to be to present what the student wants in such a way that he is able to take it. Since he has joined a language class, one must assume that he seeks some sort of language education. Anything that promises to improve the efficiency of this, as selection into more homogeneous groups does, is to be welcomed.

Yet the fact remains that in all but very large centres, and for any but the most commonly studied foreign tongues, there are neither the students nor the tutors to provide a number of parallel classes. The typical adult language class presents a group of people with wide variations in kind and force of incentive, in native ability, in educational experience, as well as in age and personal or family circumstances. The tutor must do his best for all these people under the less than ideal conditions of adult courses.

All teachers stress how important it is in learning a language to undertake continual practice. The schoolmaster counts himself seriously handicapped if his class does not have a daily period of foreign language study. The adult class, however, normally meets once a week for two hours. It would perhaps be better if it could have two meetings of one hour each, but such an arrangement would demand the sacrifice of two evenings by both tutor and student and would probably not be possible in a high proportion of cases, even if funds were available to bear the extra cost.

It is probably wise to limit the number of enrolments for a class. Efficient teaching is hardly possible with more than twenty people. If enrolments significantly exceed this figure, either a second class should be started, or the excess people turned away. To accept them all in one class, as is commonly done, is seriously to jeopardise the chances of any profiting from it.

Outside the class some members may have the time for private work, but many will not, and few will have the precious opportunity to hear and practise the spoken language. The tutor can rarely assume that his students will be able to listen to the valuable language courses broadcast from time to time, although it is a great help if he can. On the whole, he must accept that his class will have no oral practice from one week to the next. Here it should be said how useful it can be if there exists a modern language club, in whose activities the student may participate outside the class. At the University of Glasgow, Italian classes are held in close collaboration with the active Dante Alighieri Society, which exists to promote the arts and culture of Italy. In 1962–63 the student wastage in all Italian classes was 30·6 per cent compared with 55·3 per cent in French, 49·2 per cent in Spanish, 55·6 per cent in German, and 53·9 per cent in Russian.

The usual duration of a session for non-vocational adult courses is 24 weeks, which is not only a short period in which to achieve very much, but leaves the student with six months to forget what he has learnt and makes him less likely to return for further study in the following session, because he becomes discouraged by what he has forgotten. The obvious solution to this problem would appear to be an extension of language courses during the summer months, but this is unfortunately rarely possible.

The most valuable experience for students may be a stay in the country whose language they are learning. Few will need persuading to go abroad since it is with this in mind that many, perhaps most, enrol for the class in the first place. Nevertheless, not all derive from their visit as much as they might. Those who embark on the package tours now offered frequently meet only fellow-tourists and people connected with the travel industry. They thus have little opportunity to speak the foreign language. Under these circumstances much confidence and effort are required to seek out situations in which it must be used.

One solution is to recommend to students the language courses for foreigners run during the summer months by universities and centres of higher education in most countries. British universities also run summer schools abroad, which are sometimes suitable for language students, although usually only for those above the elementary level. Tutors need, however, to point out that the courses give much free time and opportunities for social activity. After all, most students want to spend their annual holiday in rest and recreation. The most effective way of improving one's command of a foreign language is to stay in a private household, as many children and undergraduates do. Tutors may help individual students to arrange this by putting them in touch with the Central Bureau for Educational Visits and Exchanges or other similar organisations.

It must be remembered that an adult's enrolment in a language class can only be taken as an indication of intention to attend for one session. As has already been said, many do not even last so long and of those that do few come back for a second year. The tutor must therefore plan his course to give the student, in 24 weeks, instruction that will have value in itself, if the student does not return for further study, and on which further study may effectively be based, if he does. Its value must not only be visible to the tutor, but above all to the student, who must be made to feel at all stages of the session that he is making progress. The stimulus given by this feeling is the one most likely to ensure that he continues his studies. He will more readily recognise his progress if it is of a practical nature; in other words, if he can use the language.

In all the circumstances the most promising aim of a beginners' class for adults in any modern foreign language will be to give the students the facility and confidence to express themselves in, and to understand simple oral speech and to understand simple written language in a limited number of everyday situations. This will not give all students what they seek, least of all examination candidates, who, in the present form of public examinations, can only be adequately prepared in a separate class. It will, however, offer an acceptable goal for the majority.

It is true that many teachers believe any such aim to be impossible of realisation. *The Teaching of Modern Languages*, published by the Incorporated Association of Assistant Masters in Secondary Schools, says in its chapter on "Those Who Start Late": "Now in two terms of some 24 hours each, there is little that a teacher can do except give advice, state the grammar with crystal clarity, suggest reading texts and gramophone records, and convince the students that all depends on them and on the work they do for themselves." All teachers of languages to adults will sympathise with the frustration obviously felt by the author of that passage, but not only is he mistaken about the amount that can be achieved, the passage betrays a fundamental error in his judgement of the way in which the tutor can help the adult. Any tutor who limits himself to grammar exposition and general advice on methods of learning deserves to lose his class—and will.

It is important that this point should be made, for, when all the unsatisfactory arrangements for adult classes are recognised, a major factor in their success or failure is still the teacher.

Many teachers, trained and accustomed to working with children or adolescents, while they agree that the student should be able to use the language, also have deeply ingrained the general premise with which the Ministry of Education Pamphlet on *Modern Languages* begins: "Whatever the claims of modern languages to an important place in the curriculum, it must be said at the outset that they cannot be justified unless the course contains intellectual discipline." This discipline is largely to be provided, in the words of the pamphlet, by "accurate written work which demands a sound knowledge of grammar". Teachers are in consequence reluctant to sacrifice accuracy or grammar.

Unfortunately, the tutor of adult beginners, because of the limitation under which he works, must be prepared to do this. With most of his non-vocational students he may at best hope to achieve in one session either accurate but halting, or inaccurate but fluent and comprehensible speech, either sound grasp of the structural basis of the language or some practical ability to use it. Many teachers appear unable to see the issue in such clear-cut terms. They feel that to leave errors of pronunciation or grammar uncorrected is to encourage bad habits, which are much more easily acquired than eradicated. In consequence, they fall between two or more stools, attempt progress over a broad field and achieve little measurable advance at all. The war-time experience of the American Army indicates that accuracy develops with wide reading and speech practice, to which fluency is the best stimulus.

In existing conditions, significant short-term progress demands a curriculum pruned with discrimination, but drastically. It is necessary to have clearly in mind a restricted goal, to which all other claims must be subordinated, even sacrificed. That suggested above is probably the most desirable, the most capable of attainment and the one that best reconciles what the subject has to offer with what most students seek. The tutor must therefore devote all his attention to making the language an instrument his beginners can use. How is he to do it?

First of all he must plan his lessons and select his material so that, if the student works conscientiously in class, he will obtain some practical knowledge of the language, even if he does no work at the subject for the rest of the week. Experience of British Army "From Scratch" courses during the Second World War indicates that some progress can be made on those terms, for teaching conditions were no better and the initial enthusiasm of the troops no greater than in the average adult class.

Nevertheless, only the irreducible minimum will be achieved in the class-room. Students must be encouraged to practise as frequently as possible outside, in order to establish firmly the locutions they have acquired in the lesson. Care must be taken to include in every class meeting material that may be worked up at home and guidance given on how to do it and on what to concentrate.

This is one justification of adopting a reading approach in beginners' classes. There are potential advantages in not introducing the class to the written language, and in teaching its sound alone. If the student had to rely solely on ear, he would associate more closely sound with meaning and develop a sensitivity to sound, as a blind person does, which would greatly assist both his own speaking and his understanding of the spoken word. He would have no difficulties of spelling, or of reconciling, in languages such as French, the sight with the sound of the word. But the student who had no tape-recorder or gramophone would be able to do no useful home practice. The value of the time that may be spent outside the class will compensate for the difficulty the student may have in linking the visual and oral images of the language. Besides, most adult students desire and require to read the language, if only public notices for tourists, as much as to speak it.

It is not, however, advisable to introduce written work for the adult beginner, certainly not in the weekly lesson. It is sufficiently difficult to train the ear and the eye to recognise and the tongue to reproduce, without trying to inculcate a fourth skill, for which, in any case, most adults will have less use.

Nevertheless, although the tutor would be wise not to recommend written exercises at home, preferring the students to memorise sentence patterns and vocabulary, he must be prepared to correct any his students may have done and find time for constructive criticism. Nothing must discourage the class from private work.

As the weekly class meeting is the only occasion on which a high proportion of students can hear and speak the foreign language, every opportunity should be seized upon for oral practice; that is, exercise of meaningful speech by the class, not by the tutor. The latter must remember, however, that it makes heavy mental and physical demands on those, the majority, who come to study after a day's work. He must allow for this by planning frequent changes of activity within the lesson, so that periods of concentrated attention are followed by more restful ones. Most tutors believe that the heaviest demand on oral participation should be made in the first half of the meeting, while the students are comparatively fresh, but after a week in which he may have had no contact with the language, the adult often needs time to warm up before he is asked to speak. If it is possible half-way through a two-hour meeting to offer a ten-minute break, the revival of energy will more than compensate for the time lost.

Always the tutor must keep a sensitive finger upon the pulse of the class. It will do more harm than good to persist in an exacting activity, if the students are too tired, or are failing for any other reason. The tutor must demand some effort, so that success brings a sense of achievement, but not too much, for the adult discouraged by failure tends not to come back.

Although fluency will take precedence over grammatical accuracy, syntax and accidence still present the most intractable problems for beginners. How much do they need to know and how should it be presented? If the tutor adheres strictly to his short-term purpose, much that is conventionally taught may be omitted. For example, in French it is of little value at this stage to introduce the 2nd Person Singular, with its concept of polite and familiar forms of address. Adult learners are unlikely to need it and its mastery requires some effort for an English speaker, to whom the concept is quite strange. No matter what the foreign language, the syntactical content of the first-year course must not exceed the minimum necessary to make it a practical, if limited, means of communication. The tutor must himself decide what that minimum is.

In the presentation of grammar it is preferable to avoid, as far as possible, rote memorisation of rules, together with lists of exceptions, and to learn carefully selected basic examples, in order to establish speech patterns as they are needed. Better that the student of German should know, "Ich werde morgen kommen", and practise its application in different contexts, than that he should know the rule about the two parts of the future tense. Even if he knows the latter, he will never make fluent use of it in speech until the pattern is established in his mind. It is not true that he will not be able to use the pattern unless he knows the rule.

However desirable it may be in principle to replace exposition of rules by examples of their working, the extent to which it is possible will depend on the class. Adults with no previous experience of language learning will probably best be taught in this way. The more formal method requires a technical vocabulary and a knowledge of sentence structure that they may not have. On the other hand, adults who have already been taught a foreign language will usually have been instructed in the more formal manner. Many are ill-at-ease and confused unless they can sum up syntax and accidence in general rules. Since both sorts of people may be found in the class, a brief enunciation of the rule, followed by intensive practice of examples of its operation, may be the best compromise.

Like grammar, vocabulary must be carefully selected. Classwork should be built around a minimum word list, of which every student should have an active command by the end of the session. The more rapid or more eager learners will supplement it, and in a number of languages students will have an additional passive vocabulary of words cognate to English, which they will recognise in reading. Where possible the vocabulary should be chosen on word frequency principles, but it should be borne in mind that some essential words will not qualify for inclusion, if frequency of use is the only criterion. In some languages word frequency lists are not readily available and tutors will have to rely on their own experience. Even where lists exist (for example, *Le Français Fondamental*, which is useful also for its list of essential grammatical points), one must be sure they are based on oral and not written usage. It is useless to bring in any word, unless it will be used in class and, more important, in life. Only frequent practice will establish it as an active part of vocabulary.

Translation, either from or into English, should not be encouraged before an advanced stage, if at all. It perpetuates that mental process from which all beginners start—recognise foreign phrase: translate into native tongue: respond in native tongue:

translate response into foreign tongue—when effective training demands that the native language be eliminated as soon as possible from the chain. Apart from this disqualification, anything that can be done by translation exercises can be done by question and answer or guided composition in the foreign language, which have the advantage of requiring that language be used as it is in life. It should, however, be noted that P. H. Hargreaves and his colleagues of Bolton Technical College, admit translation into their *French Once A Week*.[4] This is a valuable attempt to provide a suitable textbook for evening class students on the lines suggested by Hargreaves in his article on "Modern Language Classes".[5]

As readers of this article will gather, good textbooks are few. Yet to prepare a satisfactory adult course from scratch is an exceedingly heavy burden of preparation for the tutor. The best commercial courses on the lines suggested are those designed to teach language audio-visually. It is generally known that the distinguishing feature of the audio-visual method lies in the introduction of each new word or phrase in association with a visual image that conveys the meaning, and that even syntax reduced to exemplary speech patterns, is explained and established by the same method. The theory, to eliminate translation into his native tongue from the student's chain of response, is admirable. The method sometimes falters in practice, because the image does not convey unambiguously the meaning of its associated phrase. However, the true value of such a course probably does not lie so much in its audio-visual presentation as in the material it contains and the order in which it is presented. The carefully selected limited vocabulary based on word-frequency, the teaching of syntactical examples rather than rules, the emphasis, from the first lesson, on language practice in circumstances he is likely to meet, make it particularly suitable to the adult beginner.

The lucky tutor, who has the necessary accommodation, a filmstrip projector, a record-player or tape-recorder, will probably get best results from adopting an audio-visual course completely, if there is one available in his particular language. Many, perhaps most, will not be so fortunate. They will, however, find that the textbooks which form part of such courses as the Harrap-Didier ones in French and German, may be used without film-strip or record. Each frame of the film-strip is reproduced in the book in the order in which it is to be used and underneath each is printed the phrase from the sound track which is associated with it. Each lesson has one series of pictures in the form of a strip-cartoon story to introduce new vocabulary, and others to explain and establish new grammar, a summary of which is printed lesson by lesson. As the book also contains exercises and a reference vocabulary, it makes a useful course on its own, with inexhaustible material for oral practice.[6]

However nicely calculated the programme may be its success will hinge on the attitude of the class and the teacher. Unless the latter brings his students to commit themselves in public to speak the language, it will fail. The whole first-year course is a crisis of confidence, because of the reserve and reluctance to expose themselves to ridicule of the majority of adults. This is the root cause of their frequent unwillingness to participate in oral work, of their often-expressed preference for a grammar-translation approach. It is the tutor's major task to overcome this obstacle. To do so he must know his students, establish with them that sympathetic rapport, which will draw them into participation at a pace best suited to each. He must neither neglect the retiring student, nor press him too hard.

One way of drawing out students, of bringing variety to the lessons and of giving practice in life-like conditions, is to get members of the class to create short scenes round everyday situations they are likely to meet. The tutor will outline the action and leave the students to improvise the dialogue. The skilful tutor may do much to overcome the fears of the shy by the way in which he arranges rôles for them, which allow them to participate while making little demand on acting ability or linguistic fluency. Success at this level will encourage them to take larger, more demanding parts.

Here it should be said that, although adults are more self-conscious than children, and no longer perhaps enjoy acting for its own sake, they will appreciate the value and purpose of exercises of this kind. If a tutor finds his class will not respond, he should ask himself whether the fault does not lie in him. Has he the confidence of his students, do his inhibitions and his lack of faith in the exercise discourage them?

Attention has been concentrated on the first year of the adult course, because it is then that the highest wastage occurs and students who do not complete that year take little away. Moreover, the principles that apply to the first year, apply equally to the second and third. One still needs to set a clearly defined and limited goal, the over-riding aim must still be mastery of the language as a means of communication. Nothing must be allowed to distract attention from this fact, and the tutor who thinks of his course as "Language and Culture" is probably over-ambitious.

The necessary material for linguistic practice may be furnished by history, institutions and manners, the culture in fact of the people whose language is being taught, but it should not be allowed to divert effort from the prime end of the course.

Reading matter will be needed and the student may well get a sense of achievement from reading a short story by an author of literary merit such as Alberto Moravia or Thomas Mann. From an aesthetic point of view, however, second year and even most third year adult students would derive as much profit from a translation of the same work into English. Their grasp of the language is still inadequate for full appreciation. They would get more experience of the colloquial language they are likely to need from reading popular magazines. They should indeed have begun to read picture magazines, such as *Paris Match* or *Der Spiegel*, before the end of the first year.

In the main, the second and third years will employ the same methods as the first to broaden and deepen the field of knowledge, with the advantages that accrue from a class made more homogeneous by previous joint study and which already has confidence in its ability to speak in real-life situations. Some written work may usefully be introduced, a little even in class. Tutors will already have found it valuable in the first year to read aloud in the foreign language a short passage which the class have not seen, and to ask members of the class to retell it orally in their own words. Now the class may be asked to write it. Class time is, however, too precious for much to be diverted from oral work and most written exercises must be done at home. It must be remembered, though, that many students will have no time for written homework and it must not therefore be made an essential part of the course. One worthwhile exercise is for students to write short compositions, which have been intensively prepared orally in class.

After three, or more probably four, years of once a week study concentrated on that sole goal, the adult beginner may be expected to have acquired a competent oral and written command of the instrument which is a foreign language. In doing so he will have learnt much about the relationship of language and thought and how the first helps to shape the second. He will have the satisfaction and profit of a high degree of intellectual and psychological effort successfully applied. At this stage he may begin to appreciate foreign literature in the original, he may employ the language to study the culture to which it belongs. He may work further to refine and polish his linguistic command, itself a rewarding humane study. He may do none of these things and merely use his acquired skill on his annual fortnight's holiday.

In any case, his action in learning a foreign language will have a social value. Society's need for linguists is increasing, more and more people with a knowledge of foreign languages are required in economic and political life. If they are to be available in sufficient numbers, a climate must be created in which competence in a foreign language is accepted as a normal accomplishment and not an eccentricity, as at present. At the very least, successful adult education helps to do this.

NOTES TO CHAPTER VI

[1] PETER NEWMARK, Conflict in Teaching Methods, *Adult Educ.*, **XXXIV** (January, 1962), p. 238, makes such a claim and defends traditional methods of achieving its ends.

[2] C. L. M. HARDING, The Students View, *Adult Educ.*, **XXXIV** (January, 1962), p. 258, analyses the motivation of students at Bolton Technical College.

[3] Very little accurate information is available about student wastage, although Harding, *op. cit.*, gives the results of a survey on the subject undertaken at Bolton.

[4] HARGREAVES, SHELDON and FERRO, *French Once a Week* (Basil Blackwell, Oxford, 1961, Book I; 1962, Book II).

[5] *Adult Educ.*, **XXXIV** (May, 1961), p. 23.

[6] On the use of audio-visual methods for adults, see M. A. L. SCULTHORP, The Language Laboratory, *Adult Educ.*, **XXXIV** (January, 1962), p. 249.

CHAPTER VII

ENGLISH LANGUAGE AND LITERATURE

Sarah Davies

LANGUAGE

ENGLISH

"English" usually covers, in extra-mural as in school teaching, both the language and the literature. Nevertheless, although there is overlapping both in content and in method, the teaching of English as language differs radically from the teaching of English as literature. Basically it is the teaching of a skill in the use and manipulation of words in a conventional frame, and its techniques, as in the teaching of any other skill, are didactic and instructional. But literature is a form of art, and, except in the description of the structure of a poem or in the analysis of the plot of a novel, it cannot be "taught" in a formal sense but requires indirect means of communication between tutor and student and an active response to the art form from both. Language classes are thus likely to differ from literature classes in the kind of student they attract, and in the reasons for his coming.

STUDENTS

Students of language are amongst the most varied and disparate in their needs and demands, and range from foreigners and semi-literates wanting instruction in the mechanics of the language to university postgraduates interested in some of the refinements of linguistic evolution or of stylised patterns; and from the neat parcellers of argument in the art of public speaking to the commercially minded concerned to "place" the products of their "creative writing". Correspondingly, the tutors, if they are to meet all the demands, must themselves be, or profess to be, not only versatile in their wide-ranging knowledge but adaptable in their pedagogic skills.

Not a few students are prompted to attend classes in language for immediately or indirectly vocational reasons. Most of them have learnt English at school and may have a range of vocabulary—if only the passive vocabulary of the newspaper-reader—and an ability to construct grammatical sentences beyond the "basic" stage; but they are aware of professional inadequacies in an industrial and commercial world, or a political and cultural world, in which the complex use of the verbal instrument demands something more than an acquaintance with a pocket dictionary or a knowledge of how to parse a simple sentence. The newspaper itself, in bulk and reading-time easily the most powerful of language teachers, is an irritant to a citizen, not wholly naïve and bemused in his response, who has the slightest awareness of the way in which words condition his thoughts and his behaviour, and who wishes actively to recognise and to defend himself against what the words are capable of doing, and to be able effectively to use words on his own behalf.

Classes in language thus attract men and women all wanting to become more or less expertly skilled in reading and writing—in the drafting of minutes and reports, in the preparation of advertising script, in the understanding and summarising of official and legal documents, in the forms of unambiguous instruction, in reading between the lines. Their students are drawn from many fields and have very mixed backgrounds—trades union leaders, works managers, civil servants, industrial and applied scientists, local government officers, administrators, company chairmen and directors needing instruction in how to dictate confidently to secretaries, secretaries enthusiastically learning how to correct the grammar and syntax of their less literate employers.

LANGUAGE AS A SKILL

In such classes the formal content of instruction is doubtless standard for the level at which the instruction is given; but unless the students are, in a way wholly foreign to essential purpose in adult education, regarded as no more than anonymous units in a group progressing at average pace, each trailing the average or being bored by the average as best he can tolerate, the tutor must be peculiarly aware of the individual needs and accomplishments of each of his students and must adapt his methods to them. If the student is to acquire or improve his skill, his active co-operation in the use of language is essential: he must be encouraged and induced to speak words as well as to listen to them, to write them as well as to read them. This is not to put a premium on self-expression, which is only incidental to the acquisition of verbal skills, and neither speaking nor writing as such takes precedence over listening and reading: the intention of the exercises is to improve comprehension in the use of words, and to promote precision and accuracy in communication.

This means that the tutor needs time and opportunity to work as much as possible with each individual student, while bringing each student into the community of the class less for general instruction than for the improvement of skill through discussion. It also means that the tutor needs to mark scripts, on topics ranging from letter-writing to what Top People do, with an attention and an exactitude of comment beyond the normal requirements of written work—scripts, incidentally, that students write not by cajolery or coercion but through accepting them as an integral and necessary part of the course. It follows that classes in language at this elementary level should not be large; nor, desirably, should they be conducted by a tutor, however well disposed, whose accent, vocabulary, and style make him seem a foreigner to his students.

LANGUAGE AS ORATORY

At what should be a higher level but commonly is not, classes in public speaking too often are vain in their pretensions and shallow in their purpose. They incline to the encouragement of the exhibitionist and of a factitious verbal expertise that has no roots; and their product repeatedly is the un-self-critical but self-conscious public speaker whose utterances lack the spontaneity and assurance of the truly skilled. The appurtenances of public speaking— posture, intonation, voice-modulation, clarity of diction, enunciation—have their proper place in class discussion but they provide only the medium for what the speaker has to say: public speaking reaches its maturity in adult classes when what he has to say and the effectiveness in communication and persuasion of his saying it are the criteria of acquired skills in the use of language. Public speaking then becomes a modern counterpart of what formerly was called logic and rhetoric and demands, or should demand, a study as stringently exact in its way as mathematics or scientific method: it also calls for a tutor who is himself no mean public speaker, students sufficiently extrovert to lay themselves open to criticism (of style and substance) by their fellows, and a class sufficiently determined to face the rigours of intense intellectual exercise in the analysis of the language of argument.

Public speaking is not for the passive student. A close reading of Burke or T. H. Huxley is but an introduction to technique; an exploration of John Stuart Mill or J. N. Keynes only a grounding in mode; a response to the orotundities of Whitefield or Churchill the merest acquaintance with empathic persuasion. On such introductory foundations the student must himself become the speaker, sure in his knowledge, systematic and convincing in his presentation, logical in his conclusion. He proves himself before his public which is the class, and is approved through their criticism, the tutor critic-in-chief. In the average class, no doubt, the potentialities in public speaking can be only modestly pursued; but, within whatever limits, the student is always on public trial and must go as far as he is able in well-read preparation and persuasive exposition. The onus lies on the tutor to be both instructor and supervisor, guide and exemplar; and courses in public speaking become for him perhaps the most exacting of all courses in language.

LANGUAGE AS CULTURAL HISTORY

A development from a study of the use of language to a study of its nature and growth is, once grammar and syntax are well founded, possible if not usual, and classes in general philology, not merely prescriptive philology, need not be exclusively for the specialist and the sophisticate when the tutor leads his students to recognise that words have no absolute and independent existence but evolve with their use in the hands of their users. Etymology (with an incidental orthography) is then not merely of antiquarian interest but a sign of cultural history; syntax is the infinitely variable device for giving the single word significance in its context of other words: linguistics in one aspect embraces the art of verbal communication, in another the science of word roots and word construction. Beginning with such a book as Schlauch's *The Gift of Tongues*, the student may be led through Ogden and Richards's *The Meaning of Meaning*, Morris's *Signs, Language and Behaviour*, Cohen and Nagel's *An Introduction to Logic and Scientific Method*, on the one hand to Ayer and Carnap, on the other in more literary bias to the problem of style.

Once he becomes aware that the words chosen, their reverberations, and the order in which they are put, are not merely idiosyncratic variations on ways of saying the "same" thing, that a truly individual style is unique both in its sentence construction and in the full content of what it is designed to communicate, the student makes a natural transition from language to literature, and in making a distinction between the two, sees no less their interdependence.

LITERATURE

THE VERBAL MEDIUM

The tutor rarely has the opportunity in practice of leading his class through language to literature: most adult students of literature are temperamentally not interested in language but come to classes already possessing a fair acquaintance with at least some kinds of writing. Usually without insight into the nature of language, they present the tutor with a formidable task of two-fold purpose: he must lead them to discern the nature of the literary medium, and he must do so, often indirectly and derivatively, in an explication of the intrinsic content and quality of the novel, the poem, and the play.

It is trite to say that literature is an art form. It is less trite to say, and by some students it is never grasped, that literature is different in kind as an art form from music, painting or sculpture whose specific expression is there for immediate apprehension by the senses, and whose quality is always basically assessed by a judgement through the senses, however much the judgement may be influenced by a sophisticated or formalised training and experience.

There is, of course, in rhyme and rhythm, cadence and metre, a direct sonal appeal in many literary forms that matches the appeal of music; and the physical pattern of words on the printed page in much poetry, and the absence of capitals and punctuation in the work of e e cummings, have marginal visual effects; but the essence of literature does not lie in these vestments when it is expressed in words, for words as sounds or as "mounds of ink" are merely the tools of the writer in his creation of the artifact.

But words are also the catalysts of meaning, the vehicles of communication: they are allusive and evocative: they function as sign and symbol: they rouse the intellect and stir the imagination: they cradle and transmit experience—though they never offer their wares directly for the taking. As instruments, as sign or symbol, they have to be understood not merely as the dictionary defines them but also as the literary artist manipulates them for his complex derivative ends, and they are understood only when the ends are recognised as much in the reader's sympathetic response as in his intellectual assent.

Literature, because of the dual nature of the medium, is thus at once the most conventional and insubstantial of art forms, and the most devious, recondite, abstruse, refined, and sophisticated. Its quality and the richness of its content are determined—and limited—by the reader's ability to endow the words with depth of meaning and to translate the author's experience into his own: in the only public discussible sense the literary work is as good or as significant as the reader is capable of making it: until the reader finds it to be good or significant it does not exist—as literature.

THE TUTOR'S METHOD

The tutor is thus faced with a primary and central challenge: he must so arrange his words, infuse his teaching, that his students come not only to follow his theme, but through him to understand the significance or potential significance for them (in their several responses) of the literary form he explicates. This is always difficult, for he must use words to talk about words, and in the very terms of the verbal medium he cannot detach himself from the literary form as he can in a critique of painting or sculpture where the form and the medium are physically outside him, apart from him. The best he can do is to attempt on the one hand to base his judgements on objective and impersonally communicable grounds and on a candid disclosure of his principles of literary criticism, and on the other to convey to his class something of his own reactions to what he finds in significant literary form. When he overcomes the difficulties and is successful in stimulating his class, he finds himself not with a class but with colleagues: when his students find literature to have significance for them, once they respond to it, perforce they actively join him in his exploration in a community of purpose.

There are naturally varying depths of understanding, and a class may be lost if the tutor is not in sensitive rapport with his students: he may be too earnest in following a prescribed syllabus or in "reaching a standard of scholarship the subject demands"; he may be too assertive and explanatory and leave the passive students with nothing to discuss; he may be too academic and formal and remind them too forcibly of the remoteness of much of what is taught in school; his pace may be too swift, even his accent too affected or his mannerisms too distracting: all these defects are injurious to the success of any class, but they are particularly disastrous in classes in literature, where the students need to go beyond an intellectual understanding of what the tutor says, to an enthusiasm, in terms of their own sensibility, for the art he elucidates. But when the tutor shares in a common search with his students for the richness of experience that is to be found in literature, when in his contagious excitement he conveys to them a measure of what no less could be theirs, classes in literature, though never easy to conduct, are found to be as successful as any others; and, the tutor being competent, it is difficult to agree with Hoggart when he implies, in his *Teaching Literature*, that there are towns and villages where classes in literature can only be expected to fail.

THE TUTOR'S APPROACH

Whatever end he may have in mind, the tutor's approach to literature is necessarily determined by the ways in which his students are predisposed towards it. Wiltshire farmers are not concerned about the niceties of academic study but respond with interest when they meet Edith Olivier and her Wilton ladies or taste the flavour of Hardy's Wessex. Sailors of the College of the Sea become literary critics when they say that Smollett talks their language and does not romanticise like Conrad. Wordsworth is a dilettante countryman to the people of Kendal and Dumfries but Frost is worth reading because "he was a farmer and knew what mud was like". Welsh miners enrich their lives in an imaginative identification of the Rhondda and Ebbw valleys with Eliot's *The Waste Land* but find *How Green Was My Valley* loaded with a sentimental nostalgia.

Courses are prepared for classes, never classes for courses. They are means, not of demonstrating the scholarship or exhibiting the personal sensitivities of the tutor, but of providing the student with the method and the tools of scholarship and of educing and evoking a responsive and attentive attitude to words in their proper position performing their appropriate function, and of doing this as objectively and unobtrusively as possible. To say to the social realist or to the moralist that literature as literature enriches life is both meaningless and embarrassing: he looks for an overt and specific message that can be translated into action, and finds a justification for literature in the adventitious use of emotive means for practical ends. Shelley's *Men of England* is a direct incitement to rebellion. Upton Sinclair's *The Jungle* is the condemnation of a body-and-soul-destroying system. Galsworthy's *Justice* is an instrument of penal reform, Sinclair Lewis's *Babbitt* a satiric indictment of the practices and values of Middletown. Shaw and Wells are explicitly didactic in their use of the play and the novel as social and political propaganda. Orwell is patriarchal in the sweep of his moral condemnation, Huxley warningly prophetic in his detailed denunciations. Manifestly it would be aridly purist and doctrinaire to deny the quality of literature to any work solely because it carries and is intended to carry a lesson; and such a work is legitimately studied in literature classes not only because it wears the formal vestments of art (as novel or poem or play) but also because of its rational theme (a theme, moreover, that is always likely to evoke lively discussion and to help banish initial diffidence).

The tutor, nevertheless, finds little difficulty in drawing an analytical distinction between art and lesson; and few of his students are reluctant to concede that Wesker is not necessarily a good playwright because he supports the underdog, or Lawrence a poor novelist because Mrs. Grundy deplores the behaviour of his characters. The tutor's developing argument introduces the students to the relationship between intention and method, form and content, to the concept of organic unity, and to the irrelevance of a technical accuracy in the use of the incidental materials of construction of the work of art: the high moral purpose of *The Ordeal of Richard Feverel* is intrinsic and is not to be discounted because no-one now accepts Meredith's notions of a proper education; *Studs Lonigan* is to be judged a well-made and moving novel with its determinist philosophy implicit in its structure and is not to be condemned because the philosophy is not universally acceptable; *Paradise Lost* is built on a Ptolemaic cosmology, although Milton accepted the Copernican and even lived into the age of Newton; and *Ghosts* still remains a deeply moving play and retains its original dramatic intensity although Ibsen's theory of genetics is wildly wrong.

LITERATURE FOR DIVERSION

The complement to literature with a social purpose is literature for diversion and entertainment. The tutor becomes the narrator: he lectures informally and, finding that talking about the books he has enjoyed induces a vicarious enjoyment in his students, may be content to design his course along the lines of Powys's *The Pleasures of Literature*, entirely for this purpose. His method is mainly illustrative and demonstrative, in a varied and carefully planned selection of examples that allow him to convey contrast in treatment of subject (as of death in *The Wife of Usher's Well*, Keats's sonnet of fears, Emily Dickinson's *Because I could not stop for death*, Cummings's *Death is more than certain*, and Dylan Thomas's *Do not go gentle into that good night*), intention expressed in technique (as in the novels of Virginia Woolf and the plays of Arthur Miller), technique evolving from simplicity to subtlety and complexity (in Shakespeare, Eliot and Keats). In the course the tutor behaves as expositor: he appears as literary critic only in the bias of his choice and is satisfied at the end of

the course to have held the interest of his students and to have
given them, on his conducted tour, some insight into the nature
of literature.

THE NOVEL

To treat the novel as a fictional "story" is perhaps even more
acceptable as an introduction to literary meaning and values, for
most people come to literature through narrative (and nursery
rhymes). As an elementary art form the good detective story, the
plot rounded off without loose ends, the point-of-view con-
sistently maintained, the transitions of point-of-view and of time
and place skilfully and unobtrusively manipulated, is amenable
to analysis and judgement on literary principles; and the principles
it illustrates—of economy, coherence and credibility, and of word-
usage and word-sequence—are adequate, with some elaboration,
to a study of *Kidnapped* or *The Moonstone*, more formally comprehensive novels in which structural ingenuity is not the main
concern. The tutor, on such beginnings, leads the neophyte from
the entertainment of a temporary diversion to the more complex
and extensive short story or novel in which the reader is not
merely taken out of himself but becomes involved as a sensitive
inhabitant in the world of the author's construction. Sayers's
Gaudy Night (however imperfect) moves out of the *genre* of the
detective story proper into the psychological novel; Dickens, in the
less tightly knit *Our Mutual Friend* puts his plot into a richly flam-
boyant matrix of live people and live places; Simenon subordinates
action to motive and takes the reader with him in understanding
human behaviour in *The Man Who Watched the Trains Go By*.

The student becomes increasingly sophisticated and mature in
his apprehension of the use (by himself no less than by the author)
of the literary instrument: he realises that once he is involved in
the plot, once he identifies himself with at least part of the author's
creation, once in imaginative response he is caught in the experiences the author's words preserve and evoke, he is a man not
merely diverted by literature but changed by it. The tutor, not
content to describe and analyse shape and pattern, but concerned to probe to heart and essence through the formal "appearance", imposes sharper criteria on his students and expects them

to extend their range of literary values and judgements: Becky
Sharp is more acutely delineated, has wider implications for and
deeper influence on the reader, than Lucy Manette; the formal
austerity of Compton Burnet is the vehicle for a different kind of
novel from *Barchester Towers* or *The Return of the Native*, and
being different in purpose is therefore different in style and
structure; *Gone with the Wind* may be an exciting and com-
petently told tale but is wholly without the depth and subtlety
and universal significance of *The Egoist*.

In his deeper judgements, intellectually applied to intention,
technique and form, emotionally measured in the degree of his
empathic commitment, the student begins to sense the overwhelming importance of literature as a moral and political
influence, not in the crude and obvious hammering of doctrine or
message but in the revelation of and comment on the human
condition. He appreciates the rôle of the President of the Im-
mortals in the tragedy of Tess and the subtler implications of the
rôle of the Comic Muse in depriving Sir Willoughby Patterne of his
"dainty rogue in porcelain". He discerns why Jane Austen, Henry
James, even the turgid Faulkner, have greater depths than Scott
and Dos Passos and Maugham. He accounts the explicit if generalised morality of Sartre or Graham Greene of less significance than
the intrinsic disclosure of the springs of human conduct in George
Eliot, Virginia Woolf or Katherine Mansfield. Discriminatingly
attentive as he reads and alert to technical complexities as he dis-
sects structure and apprehends the unity of "perfect" form, he is
prepared at last to commit himself to the stimulus of a short story or
a novel that apparently is without the traditional tale or orthodox
"plot" although it is steeped in a concentrate of experience—on the
one hand in the expressionist turbulence of Wolfe's *Of Time and the
River* and in the laconic intensity of Hemingway's narrative metaphors, on the other in the classical precision of Joyce's *The Dead*
and the richly formal tightly coherent complexity of his *Ulysses*.

THE FORMALISM OF THE POEM

The allusive, evocative and symbolic content of much "prose"
is not lost on the discerning student; nor does he fail to realise that
narrative, even in the most tenuous form, is subordinated to other

purposes in such novels and short stories as *Ulysses* and *The Dead*, *The Garden Party*, *The Ordeal of Richard Feverel*, and *The Sound and the Fury*. He may accord a place to recognisable verse in at least some plays, and not find himself brought to the surface of an unselfconscious immersion by finding prose in a context of blank verse in *As You Like It* or *The Tempest*, poetic devices in a prose context in *St. Joan*, or ballads in *Sergeant Musgrave's Dance*. But unless he is already an addict he often faces the tutor with an initial and ingrained resistance that makes him always reluctant to follow courses that include poetry, or drives him away when poetry is too directly forced upon him. This widespread allergy derives from two main sources: the extremely artificial structure of most poetry and the obliquity of the poetic purpose.

Commonly the tutor, no less than the student, takes prosody for granted. Rhyme and its permutations; assonance and onomatopoeia; rhythm becoming laden with heavy beat or becoming variable and syncopated; verse patterns; cadence and stress and the linking of spoken words in felicitous sonal sequences, sense not destroyed in the sequence: all these contribute to what "everyone" recognises to be the anatomy of poetry, and make poems recognisable as poetry by the sonal (and printed) shape. But, being taken for granted, they are not to be neglected in discussion in a naïve acceptance or supposition that poetry in its essence is represented in the shape, or that the shape defines the poetry; for it requires no great sensibility to see that despite the mechanical perfection of the shape, the stuffed owl is sometimes not far away. They are to be extracted, sensed, analysed, savoured, weighed, approved for what they do and how they do it; and are to be recognised as multiple and complex devices that place words as signs and symbols in a "musical" setting designed not to give verbal information but to evoke mood.

The student's attention is drawn to the elements of "music" when the tutor refers to simple stress or rhyme, and the beat of *The Charge of the Light Brigade* or *How They Took the Good News* gives a gusto to the recitation that no-one can miss. It is less easily "shown" when the strict rigidity of a formal, traditionally sanctified rhythm is overlain by a staggered pulse arising when the words as sense demand their own individual or phrasal emphasis that is in harmonic relationship with the expected beat:

in *The Windhover* or *The Wreck of the Deutschland* the coherence is overt, but *The Journey of the Magi* demands more from the student, if its "meaning" in its form is not to elude or bewilder him, than a simple ability to place accent where it should fall. The shape of a Shakespearean sonnet is superficially ancestral to a Miltonic but the diction no less than the intention of the two poets determines a whole difference in technique and temper (regardless of what the poem is "about") that arises from the different ways in which the prototypic sonnet form is manipulated.

A study of prosody of this kind is clearly not to be aridly academic. No student should be expected to enjoy analysis merely for the purpose of taking the machine to pieces: he becomes interested only as the pattern contributes to his apprehension of the "meaning" of poetry when the words are couched in the frame of the poem. When the student realises that the "meaning" of a poem is to be sought in its pattern and to be found in his response to it, then he is in a position to go further when the traditional form, itself a product of centuries of evolution along multiple lines, is modified, adapted, elaborated, replaced by "experimental" poets who attempt novel effects not for the sake of the novelty (and not to be judged good or bad merely as novelty) but for the increased depth of significance they can give to their words in new sonal, rhythmic contexts.

WORDS AS SYMBOLS

The formal pattern is essential to "pure" poetry; and a poetic bemusement is incipiently evoked even when the words are in a language not understood, or in words (*'Twas brillig*) that are only quasi-referential, or in semantic and syntactical condensations and inversions (*anyone lived in a pretty how town*) that slide away from the tripping metre. Nevertheless, the poetry does not lie in the pattern, which in great part can be objectively assessed and thus easily "taught", but in the words that make the pattern—words used as signs and symbols, grammatically arranged, meaningful as literature and not merely as vehicles for sound. The tutor's task is onerous in attempting to convey to his students something of what poetry is designed to do in this verbal sense, and (in not making his exposition a series of comments *in vacuo* on an abstracted "nature of poetry") to give his words point by discussing actual poems in illustration. Such exploration emphasises the deviousness of poetic purpose and the highly subjective recognition of what is significant in poetry, significant not because of its publicly communicable content as record or report but because of its powers of penetration to depths of feeling whose probing is the self-sufficient measure, offered therefore for singularly personal endorsement, of its quality.

The tutor is thus able to talk only around the poem, explicating the relative triviality of allusion in unusual words or word-associations, referring analogies (imagery, metaphors, conceits) to their historical or local contexts, suggesting sources when they can be found, generally removing the obstacles that arise from the student's ignorance, or misinterpretation, or obliquity of understanding. He distinguishes between an apparent simplicity of structure and a complexity of content in *London, My life closed twice, Sunday Morning*, or *The Second Coming*, or, conversely, reveals the poverty of content that underlies a load of pretentious simplicity in *Simon Lee*. He exposes the second-hand or the synthetic sentiment, the merely decorative simile, the maladroit felicity that leads only to the banal, the debasement of words to sounds, the exploitation of the expected, the repetitious trick. He encourages the student to be continuously alert to and aware of the criteria applied in judgement of the poem and their propriety to the kinds of poems judged; and, in an exploration of how they evaluate poetry, tutor and student together formulate standards less in a definitive "classical" mould than in the functional appositeness of instrument to need, and meet the new and the untried with relative freedom from a prejudice resting on a traditional orthodoxy.

SUBTLETIES IN WORD-USAGE

A narrative poem is often a tale told to be remembered: its versification, as in the ballad, is designedly an adjunct to memory, and its content is history or myth to be re-experienced with emotional overtones. As narrative it commonly is basic to the epic which demands that the reader be not only involved in the unfolding of the "events" but responsive to them in ways determined by the poet-narrator. In both kinds of poem, the words are to be understood partly in their referential sense, and while in association they may be highly charged, in isolation they may not always carry the burden of allusion that makes *The Waste Land* such a long short epic. In their "classical" form, many long didactic poems—*Essay on Man, The Deserted Village, The Prelude*—use words in the same kind of referential way and ask from the reader a response weighted towards a controlled intellectual approval in which the sentiments are explicit and in great part available for public discussion; and (on the assumption that their wide-ranging vocabulary is understood) the student can be expected to grasp their meaning without too much introspection.

On the other hand, in much of what is regarded as "pure" poetry, the link between frame and content is tight and essential and the purpose not to report or record or discuss or philosophise but to embody feelings in words. Superficially, as in *The Rime of the Ancient Mariner*, the poem may still carry a tale, but few students fail to grasp that the tale is wholly secondary; and in a Miltonic epic the use of a formidable diction is scarcely more misleadingly a sign that the poet and not the schoolmaster is speaking. The lyric is a "spontaneous" expression of delight however carefully contrived; and the formal precision of a Shakespearean sonnet is the only proper manner of cradling the timeless sentiments of verbalised emotion.

There is obvious difficulty in any attempt by the tutor to inspire in the student a direct enthusiasm for the poem (and not for the tutor's enthusiasm for the poem) when the central measure of the poetic quality lies in the reader's response; and assertion and encouragement can be misplaced if the student becomes guiltily conscious that he ought to like the poem when he is not even sure that he "understands" it. The difficulties grow in much of modern poetry when poets, becoming increasingly devious and skilful in their techniques, are also increasingly private in their word-associations and evocations; and even when they are not exploratory to the limits of faint allusion they express a highly personal experience with almost no bond of community in word-usage, imagery and idiom between them and their (common) reader. The tutor, taking his students on a voyage through what

may be the "mind" of poets, is always frustrated by an ignorance
of the psychology of verbal symbolism and must remain satisfied,
however dissatisfied, trusting to nature and the muse for his
students' final understanding, response, and delight in what the
poets do.

RIGHT WORDS IN RIGHT SEQUENCE

The full interest of the student is engaged when he places words
as sign and symbol in their prosodic frame and finds the meaning
of the poem to lie in his apprehension of its total form. He discovers the poet to be an isolate, eremitic until there is community
of response; and he comes to sense that the quality of the poet's
experience, as embodied in the poem, can be matched in him only
when his own experience actual or psychological, parallels the
poet's. How he reads poetry depends on the intimacy of his
knowledge of words, on his ability to analyse or at least to recognise
the form of the poem, on his acquaintance with the place of
the poem in its context of other poems similar in theme and in
form; but above all on the kind of man he is and his ability in his
own reconstructive imagination to relive with the poet the
occasion for the poetry.

Much literature is thus not for the persistently immature. The
tutor, affected unavoidably by the "new criticism", emphasises
the poem itself, and although he necessarily concentrates on the
discussible—on the whole technical scheme analysed into its
poetic elements—he expects his students to carry their comprehension into an apprehension of what the technique is designed
to do in a recondite proliferation. He is not satisfied with a simple
acknowledgment of the plain imagery of

Petals on a wet black bough

or with a simple pleasure in *My heart leaps up*, still less with an
approval of the overt comparisons within *Fair daffodils* and *To
Daffodils*. Nor does he involve his students sufficiently when he
takes them through the formal construction of *Drink to me* and
Auld Lang Syne and *Oh ! To be in England*.

The tutor must probe with his students the intrinsic nature of
the tightest and most rigidly organised of literary forms to reach
the heart of poetry, until they understand why Shakespeare and

Milton, Keats and Wordsworth reserve the sonnet for their most intense experiences; in its closed structure, moulded to a formal precision, they find the one perfect instrument for the embodiment of universalised emotion. Reaching this pitch of maturity, the student, applying a modified version of Richards's "practical criticism", recognises in both intellectual and emotional response the propriety of the work of art, finds the words in prosodic and semantic sequence to be immutable, echoes in empathy the inner coherence of sentiment and content, and acknowledges in multiple judgement his conviction of its innate truth.

The routes to the inner sanctum are of course varied and devious. Nursery rhymes lead the way to *If I should ever by chance grow rich*, most of de la Mare and much of Yeats. Moving through the ballad's emphatic sonal tale to the glancingly allusive narrative of *La Belle Dame sans Merci* and *Christabel*, the tutor avoids over-simplification by contrasting their lyrical quality and the rich romantic overtones of *The Eve of St. Agnes* with the poly-semantic satire of *The Rape of the Lock* and the dramatic involu-tions of *My Last Duchess* and *Soliloquy in a Spanish Cloister*. Or he may contrast the poetic embellishments of the semantic core in poems of different temper, setting Augustan against Romantic in a clash between Pope's

> Know then thyself; presume not God to scan:
> The proper study of Mankind is Man.

and Coleridge's violent rejoinder:

> Ignore thyself—and strive to know thy God.

Extending his theme he delineates theories of critical relativism in Jonson's and Dryden's disparagement of Shaksepeare's "art", Keats's attack on the rocking-horse verse of the Augustans, Arnold's attack on Shelley, Byron and Keats for their anarchy, Eliot's early attack on Milton for fouling the stream of English poetry—and his later recantation; and at the same time discusses derived approaches to the poem as a self-subsistent organic composition containing within itself the criteria on which it is to be judged. In the contemporary synthesis of classical and romantic criticism the tutor demonstrates the evaluating of a poem in terms of the poet's "realised intention" in the "perfection" of its structure.

Alternatively, the tutor may follow the line of the Joycean "aesthetic transaction" from lyric through epic to drama. In *The Revenge, The Ride of Paul Revere, Sir Patrick Spens*, the student hears the same delight that marks *Jenny kissed me* and *Loveliest of trees*; but in following the tale he realises that the emotion generated by its telling resides only partly in the "events", which are clothed in a metre no less evocative (or no less adequately complementary) in its effects. If the student further compares *Kublai Khan* and *The Lady of Shalott* he finds the narrative fading to the ghost of a tale and he is left with the "vague suggestiveness" of Poe's "genuine poetry"—a highly wrought symbolism.

In variant approach, the narrator in ballad and epic is seen as the poet muted: consciously (as for Eliot) the poet seeks the final detachment of the dramatist in his search for a cosmic universality, and in an expansion of vision and purpose transcends the recording of events, even the highly important "events" of a passionate but personal experience, as he attempts to focus an all-seeing eye on the central significance of life.

The lyric cry—Joyce's "simplest verbal vesture of an instant of emotion"—is heard in *Chamber Music*, caressed in *Words*, isolated in the Imagist poem, concentrated in the sonnet, transmuted in *Ode to the Confederate Dead*, transcended in the epic, and lost in the drama. It dominates Milton's early poems, changes through his sonnets into the narrative voice of *Paradise Lost* and merges into the protagonist's in *Samson Agonistes*. Keats moves smoothly from the self-confessions of *I stood tiptoe* to the impersonal *Ode to Autumn* and the relative objectivity of *Hyperion*. Browning, after his heart-on-sleeve *Pauline* identifies his voice with that of duke, or bishop or monk, and smothers his dismay at the indifference of the world in the projections of *The Ring and the Book*.

Accompanying the poets, the student finds a flood of meaning in Eliot's "objective correlative"—and in doing so identifies Eliot's ambivalent response to Milton by making a comparison between *Paradise Lost* and *The Waste Land* in terms of diction, compactness, moral purpose, and literary intention. Eliot's "three voices of poetry", echoing Joyce in objective terms, are followed from his songs through his epic to *Murder in the Cathedral* and the intensely conscious craftsmanship of *The Cocktail Party*. Shakespeare is then recognised as the artist who infuses Joyce's "aesthetic transaction" with final truth: from sonnets through narrative poems to plays he take the ultimate step towards the complete detachment, the depersonalising, of the artist in an "objective correlative" that becomes the one social form amongst all the forms of literature. With Joyce, tutor and student discover that in the "splendid detachment of drama" only two elements of the "transaction" remain—the image and the audience, for the artist, supreme as creator, "has been refined out of existence".

THE PLAY

The frame of poetry commonly lies in the unit poem; but when the tutor reveals the quality of poetry to lie less in the frame, which can be rigidly orthodox and traditional, than in the closeness and intimacy of the verbal effect, he breaks down in his students the conventional barriers of a classification of literary artists into novelists, poets and playwrights. While not many novels are instilled with the spirit of poetry and none is written in verse, a great many plays, especially those of the Elizabethans and Jacobeans, use poetry as an intrinsic instrument and reach an intensity of emotion—and promote the action of the play— precisely because they adapt the high concentration of experience in poetry to dramatic ends. Some plays directly invite study for their verbal content—a few, like *Samson Agonistes* and most of the plays of the Romantics only for their verbal content—when they can be ignored as stage plays.

Combined with the physical difficulty of producing a play in class, this academic approach thus has an ambivalent content. It sways between a concentration on the eye-read words, the text, the structure, the Aristotelian unity, the levels of meaning, the literary significance of the play; it may even include discussion on the origins, the historical context, the contemporary fashion in which the play was written, perhaps the circumstances of the actors, the staging, and the contemporary theatre audience; it may go yet further in an assessment of the emphases, settings and production of the play at different times and places by different producers. But it is a study always in the class-room, is conducted wholly in discussion, and reduces the play to a text: it is not a study of the play as played.

In broad division the tutor has two alternative paths to follow in his exposition and analysis. In the tradition of scholarly textual criticism he induces his students to make a close study of the written play, its shape, the quality of its diction, the relationship between action and character, the nature of the characterisation, the interlocking relevance of plot and sub-plot, and the integration of the dramatic elements into a structural unity. He explores alternative readings, compares one kind of interpretation with another, looks for an underlying philosophy of dramatic art, finds an embodiment of standards of art in what the writer has made, and generalises his theme to embrace drama, dramatic theory, and criticism. According to his bent, the kinds of students he has, his particular purpose in the class as he finds it, he makes his study comparative and historical, setting side by side the Cleopatra theme of Shakespeare, Dryden and Shaw and the "waiting" theme of Odets and Beckett, for contrasting attitude, technique and purpose, *The Crucible* and *The Devils*, *The Duchess of Malfi* and *Macbeth* for modes of manipulating tragedic theme, Congreve and Sheridan, Wilde and Coward for light on the comedy of manners and the world of wit, Osborne, Wesker and Pinter for obliquities of protest. He may decide that in a brief course it is impossible to organise the classwork to give students a sound knowledge through reading the large number of plays of many different kinds, times, and authors, necessary for a comparative study that is likely to be meaningful, and he concentrates with even greater scholarly intention on the quality of at most a few plays, sometimes only one hypercharged play—*Hamlet* or *St. Joan* or *A Long Day's Journey into Night*—in the belief that the manner of analysis and the canons of judgement that emerge from such an intense and exacting study are much more precise, penetrating, significant and illuminating than are to be got from a relatively superficial ranging over too many plays of too many different types, pointing out that specific dissection of one or two "good" plays serves as a guide to method that is then applicable generally to all plays by the intelligent student.

There can be no doubt that such studies are both proper and profitable. They are, moreover, traditional and long-tried, and are the orthodox studies of school and university. They ensure that students know a great deal about plays through approved methods, and are capable of evaluating plays as constructs, and as the verbal embodiment of experience. Nevertheless, they are studies in the class-room, they suppose that a play can be understood in much the same way as a novel or a poem, they generalise an attitude to words that makes the words have self-contained "meaning", they make the tacit assumption that all plays are like *Prometheus Unbound*—as though the score were the music and the architect's plans the building. But a play as a play is only secondarily to be talked about: it is not a play until it is played: it is primarily "drama" with activity at its core: it is to be seen and heard as it is acted, intricate and complex in multifarious ways as the novel and the poem are not, with a verbal text that is merely the foundation on which the elaborate superstructure of the production is reared, and with dramatic qualities that can be directly experienced only in the live performance. This is an aspect of literature that is far too central and important to be neglected in extra-mural work, and one that the tutor is compelled sooner or later to acknowledge.

The naïve student looks on the play as being as static as the novel and the poem. He "knows" Shakespeare only as a poet although he thinks of him as a playwright: the nearer he gets to the text the further he gets from the play. He finds Jonson tedious, and difficult to understand, and is never remotely aware of the stagecraft that gives significance to his acting-script. Even when he visits the theatre he commonly supposes that he is offered undeformed *King Lear* or *The Rivals* or *Candida*. He is surprised to find that Shakespeare's plays are more than a series of soliloquys or declaimed sonnets. He has never asked himself when studying the play what the words mean in terms of "stage business": he examines nouns and adjectives rather than verbs, never looks, as an actor must, for the pattern of every speech (however short it may be), never finds the shape and length of every word as well as its sound and never tries to reproduce them. He misses the dramatic essence of the plays of Shakespeare and Jonson because he does not realise that they earn their place in the history of dramatic art not for reasons that commend them to the academic critic (although these are not to be neglected) but because of the

E

"actable", the stage qualities of their plays which class-
room examination and discussion can only partly explain
and may even—as in Lamb's criticism of Shakespeare—explain
away.

He appreciates the likeness in temper of the soliloquy to the
sonnet but unless he is aware of the full dramatic context of the
soliloquy he may never notice that its intention is in marked
contrast to that of the poem, and that this intention is to be found
within the text itself: he has to know what to look for before he
can see it. The reflective significance of the sonnet is contained
and confined often within the "when-then" frame of thought, but
the soliloquy represents only a temporary withdrawal from the
action (a withdrawal "made flesh" on the Elizabethan stage by
the isolating of the soliloquiser and so the concentrating of
attention upon him) so that its significance may be assessed and
the next step in the action prepared effectively as demonstrated
in Hamlet's unanswered question.

Part of the student's difficulty, whose removal becomes the
tutor's difficulty in the teaching, is to realise that what he sees
and hears in the theatre is unique to the occasion—in the production, the lighting and the sets, the rotes of acting, the minutiae
of each actor's speech and movement, the interpretation, the
apprehension of the audience, the environmental conditioning of
the student as he sits in the theatre, even what the critics say:
Joan Littlewood is not Tyrone Guthrie, Redgrave is not Olivier,
a Monday audience is not a Saturday audience, a Glasgow response
is not a Bristol response, Stratford is not The Aldwych. The play
in its variant nuances is thus what on the given occasion is acted
before the audience, and until it is acted, and until there is a
responsive audience, it cannot well be said to be a play. Even
when acted (as in rehearsals, for instance) it is barren in its central
purpose to stimulate, provoke and involve an audience which, as
it finds itself committed and in the process of committal gives the
play a reality, brings it to life, in the only dramatic significance it
can have. This is what Styan means when, in *The Elements of
Drama*, he says that a play is "the response of an audience to its
performance"—an assertion that appears perverse when it is taken
literally but that in its context emphasises the essential participation of the audience in any full concept of the play as an art form,

and that rightly insists on the indivisibility of auditorium and stage in the construction of the theatre.

There are inevitable complications in bringing the acted play into the extra-mural class that must be resolved in novel ways: the formal two-hour sessions must be disrupted or supplemented by theatre visits (by the whole class together); the plays the tutor wishes to study must be available in local production, or conversely the course must be devised to revolve around the appropriate plays available; the techniques of production, the intricate organisation behind the public performance, can be authoritatively explained only in lectures by visiting professionals—producers, actors, playwrights, designers, critics; discussion and written work by the class are desirably direct and immediate dramatic criticism, and need to be integrated with the tutor's over-riding theme of the course; and the course itself can often be integrated only with strain when a sequence of locally available plays is without coherence either in kind or in production. The mechanics of arranging theatre visits can be troublesome, especially in the small town; and the administrative burdens that fall upon the tutor can be heavy.

Nevertheless, the difficulties are rarely insurmountable, and are offset by the enormous gains to students and tutor when a class is stirred from its usual sessile passivity. In the liveliness of giving to the play their joint part in the play's fulfilment, the students not merely gain an immediate enrichment of their understanding of the play: they also discover literature to be not something outside them, to be "learned" with diffidence and uncertainty but to be an experience to relish in the active enjoyment of it. And in thus directly apprehending the quality of the play they more readily open themselves to an understanding of the poem and the novel as literary forms that no less they can enter into and assimilate in ways equally penetrating.

PURPOSE

The tutor needs a lifetime to do all he would wish to do in a single extra-mural class in literature; but it is not beyond the bounds of the possible for him to show the pattern of the literary art form to be woven of a myriad strands, separable in dissection but a unity as constructed. He weans his students from an ephemeral being-taken-out-of-themselves, moulds his exposition to their enlightenment, and leads them to a refined and sophisticated awareness that in the fusion of matter and manner, profound intention fulfilled by expert technique, the novel or the poem or the play is, when it is "perfect", at once inevitable in its construction, satisfying in its intellectual and emotive content, a harmony of inter-related parts, and a catalyst of experience radically transforming in their nature the students who "complete the course".

CHAPTER VIII

ART AND MUSIC

Martin Baillie and T. B. Wilson

ART—MARTIN BAILLIE

METHODS OF ART HISTORY

The study of art need not be a historical study but in adult education the historical approach is generally adopted, either in a narrow, art-historical sense, concerned with changes in style, or taking a wider view in seeing these changes within a general-historical development. When art-studies made their debut in adult education, they chose, or as it might seem, were obliged within the traditions of the movement, to clothe their nakedness in the garments of social science. There were lectures upon art and society and courses, which cruising from Giotto to Picasso or anchored in the quattrocento, emphasised the relation of art to the contemporary social structure. Considering the complexity of the subject and that tutors could rarely specialise in any one period, it must often have been handled in rough and ready fashion. Yet however primitive its methods and conclusions, art was thereby introduced to a wider circle of students, established as a normal, intelligible activity and discussion promoted on its nature and purpose. As adult education has broadened to embrace a wide range of subjects there has been less concern with the socially determined character of art.

However, this is not simply a consequence of a more catholic adult education, nor of the fact that art, having established its social roots, could now withdraw into its own autonomous activity, but a reflection of developments in art-historical research. Wolfflin's exclusively formalistic method at the turn of the century had yielded between the two wars to a method which paid maximum attention to general history, drawing upon specialised studies in social and political history and the history of ideas. In recent years there has been a marked turning away from what has been called sociological interpretation.

Antal's *Florentine Painting and its Social Background,* an example *par excellence* of the sociological method was published in 1946. In his *Hogarth and His Place in European Art* published posthumously in 1962, there is greater emphasis, though without abandonment of the sociological method, upon the internal world of art, the influences upon Hogarth of previous artists and his influence upon those who came after him—the titles of the two books are themselves indicative of the change. We can accept the author's explanation "that whereas readers of the earlier book are not necessarily informed on events and thoughts in fourteenth century Florence, most English speaking peoples have a fairly good idea of eighteenth-century England", and yet sense a change in the direction of Antal's thought. Hauser's *Social History of Art,* 1951, was succeeded by his *Philosophy of Art History,* 1958, where in the opening chapter he considers the scope and the limitations of the sociological method. Gombrich in *The Story of Art,* 1955, traced developments in pictorial representation against a background of social change. In the Mellon Lectures of 1956 (published as *Art and Illusion,* 1960), this had become a study in the "psychology of representation" which "does not aim at upsetting the previous interpretation but at justifying it and refining it in the light of contemporary work in psychology".

Art and Illusion, Art and Visual Perception, Psycho-analysis of Vision and Hearing, all of them important works published within the last eight years are indicative of increasing reference to specialist studies in psychology and psycho-analysis as against sociology and social history.

What is to be noted, however, is not simply the adoption of a psychological as against a sociological approach, but a new emphasis upon the work of art itself, upon pictorial representation, the organisation of shapes and colours upon a canvas. It is difficult to resist the suggestion that this is, in part at least, a direct consequence of developments in painting, which after a brief period of social comment in the immediate post-war period have entered a phase where meaning is locked within the formal arrangement, as in the expressive gesture of action painting.

Gombrich's *Art and Illusion* is in a sense a continuation of

Wolfflin's formalistic methods along fresh lines. In its concern with pictorial representation it may be argued that it shows a reactionary turning back to *l'art pour l'art*. This would be incorrect. The "sociological interpretation of cultural achievements", to use Hauser's phrase, has become a part of our culture forming a persistent hinterland to whatever enquiry is conducted. It is worth remarking here that Stokes' psycho-analytic essay on Michelangelo has little in common with Freud's 1910 essay on Leonardo. Freud's essay shows little concern with the unique qualities of Leonardo's work; it is precisely these qualities in Michelangelo's work which Stokes emphasises. Yet Freud's study is largely antipathetic to a sociological interpretation whereas Stokes' succeeds in "justifying and refining it".

The work of art is many sided, offering different aspects according to the angle at which it is viewed. In imaginative response we may grasp its totality but intellectual enquiry is obliged to adopt fixed standpoints where certain aspects are revealed and others remain hidden or distorted by the angle at which they lie.

All of this is important to art-studies as these are conducted in adult education. Whilst the sociological method has been the dominant and most fruitful art-historical method for many years, it cannot be said that it has been everywhere adopted in adult education. Some tutors have adopted it, others have fought shy of doing so either because they felt ill-equipped to make use of it or because they mistrusted its findings and procedures. Yet its influence has been felt everywhere and has perhaps prevented the emergence of varied lines of enquiry with distinct objectives and appropriate methods of enquiry. The study over twenty meetings of an historical period in art, Dutch Portraiture of the seventeenth century, painting of the Italian Renaissance, the Florentine Quattrocento, Post-Impressionism, Twentieth Century painting, has concealed a vagueness of approach. There are, after all, many questions which can be asked about any historical period.

Moreover, it is doubtful whether the period study can meet all needs. Certainly the broad survey of European art with its generalisations, attempts to introduce every figure of consequence and illustrations appearing and disappearing with the rapidity of targets in a shooting gallery, is no encouragement to further study, but some story of art, ranging over several centuries, should provide the necessary basis for the more advanced study of a specific period.

It is a common supposition that the story of art is essentially one of increasing skill in the representation of appearance, that Leonardo was trying to do what Rembrandt did without quite succeeding. On this reckoning art is always moving, sometimes slowly, at other times in leaps, towards illusion, the creation of three dimensional space and the unambiguous disposition of figures within that space, the rendering of figures with anatomical accuracy, the realisation of different textures such as wood, stone, hair, cloth, flesh. It is true, of course, that there is such a story and it can very properly be told, but one can also follow the astonishing twists and turns in the representation of space, the approaches to and subsequent departures from natural fact which give a truer picture of its development and greater insight into its nature.

In advanced work it is desirable to provide an alternative to the study of a period, valuable though that is, taking a broader chronological view perhaps in intensive study of a few important pictures from various periods, not with a view to summing up the developments through several centuries, but giving fresh insights into particular works and the traditions to which they belong.

The description, analysis and interpretation of a work of art has to cope with several elements in interaction. There are shapes, colours, lines of direction which are in themselves affective but resolved into the appearance of natural forms—an old woman reading, a child with a doll, a nude woman, apples upon a kitchen table, the interior of a church, a winter landscape, a woman mourning a dead child—attain a meaning which, though ambiguous as in all artistic expression, has its own kind of precision. A Venus by Botticelli has a different meaning from one by Boucher, this can be partly but not entirely understood in the attitudes and from the physical appearance of the figure. The whole theme and formal arrangement, however, can only be further elucidated with reference to the institutions, customs and ideas of the age and place in which it was painted—not all Pater's attentiveness to the nuances of Botticelli's drawing could reveal the neo-Platonic symbolism of the Primavera. A work of art is born of an artistic tradition and can only be understood in relation to that tradition: the tradition is itself part of a greater whole. No tutor, however erudite, can follow up every line of enquiry which a work of art invites, but by working within the limits of his knowledge he can bring himself and the student to the point of possible affective response. In this response the work of art of whatever period is of our time and our place; we interpret it in terms of our own attitudes and ways of life. And this, though not the only, is the essential purpose of art-education.

ARTS AND FINE ARTS

Education in art tends to be exclusively education in the fine arts or beautiful arts (*les beaux arts, die schöne Kunst, le belle arti*) to use the term which distinguished them from the useful arts. There is room for classes in the crafts, or in the arts and crafts considered together, and of course that twentieth-century development of craft, industrial design, both for itself and in respect of its links with modern painting, is a proper subject in adult education. Students who some years ago attended the rococo exhibition in Vienna, where painting and sculpture were exhibited along with furniture, jewellery and pottery, were given an insight into the rococo style which can never be given in a study of painting and sculpture alone.

Not only the arts and crafts can be usefully studied in relation to one another but just as significantly art, music, architecture and literature. This can be done as a quasi-sociological pursuit but even more to allow one art form to cast light upon another. Comparisons have to be made with care and with regard to the different pace of developments within each art. Moreover, it must not be forgotten that they are distinct modes of expression whose unique qualities must not be lost sight of in the attempt to find common ground. Two courses, Art and Music in the Romantic Period, and Twentieth Century Art and Music, attended by students with advanced knowledge of one or other subject showed resistance to any blurring of these distinctions. Joint courses of this nature are likely to be exceptional; it is rare to find a tutor capable of tackling a subject which demands considerable knowledge of two art forms. In the courses mentioned above two tutors were in attendance at each class meeting.

It is clear that television has affected adult reading habits even if it is uncertain as to what precisely has happened. In education visual aids have extended to a wide variety of subjects and have become not so much aids to verbal learning as a distinct way of learning. Art education has of course made use of visual aids over a long period, but, ironically enough has been slow to grasp the opportunities offered by a revolutionary development—the availability of colour-slides made directly from paintings and sculptures in the churches and museums of Europe and the United States.

The colour-slide has now ousted the black-and-white slide. There was, often enough among the most scholarly and conscientious tutors, an initial reluctance to use it. The principal arguments were firstly, that the colour-slide was less accurate than the black-and-white within its limitations—an objection which was speedily overcome by improvements in colour photography; secondly, that the increased verisimilitude was likely to confuse the student as to the difference between reproduction and the original. It would lead, it was said, to an impoverished connoisseurship and this is a criticism which has, of course, been made also of the use of black-and-white photographs. Whether it applies any more strongly to colour is doubtful; certainly the black-and-white photograph can create its own particular confusion. A student who had attended a course on Eighteenth Century Painting illustrated in black-and-white slides remarked, when confronted with Hogarth's "Marriage à la Mode" on the walls of the National Gallery, "I always thought they were in black and white". Many students of High Renaissance painting who are acquainted with the Sistine Chapel ceiling only in black-and-white reproduction (it is rarely reproduced in colour) think of it as being in black-and-white, and not as a painting in colours of which they have seen only a black-and-white reproduction. The fact that high-quality reproduction may persuade the student, temporarily at any rate, that he is looking at an original is to be welcomed in that it indicates a sharpened response however mistaken in certain particulars—scale, for instance. The poor quality of slides which were not only photographs of photographs but of photogravure reproductions avoided confusion with, but offered little information on, the originals and must have blighted many a budding interest in art.

The objections to the colour-slide are largely a thing of the past. Whatever the disadvantages of studying art in photographic reproduction the practice has come to stay: the disadvantages if they cannot be overcome can be minimised by increasing accuracy of the reproduction. One hopes that the student will never be blind to the gap between reproduction and original and will respond before an original work to these qualities which the original alone possesses. Students in Glasgow as in other cities have ready access to any number of fine paintings and visits arranged, for example, to Florence, following upon a course in Florentine painting, have ensured that a number of students know original works from the period studied. Whether courses should be arranged in centres where students have little chance of seeing originals is debatable.

In teaching art to adults, a slowness in grasping the possibilities offered by the high-quality slides of today is related not so much to the initial resistance to colour, but to the continuing use of the slide in a marginal rather than a central position. Art education was for a long time, of necessity, verbal rather than visual in its method and many a tutor has felt dissatisfied in this respect, judging that it encouraged students to read about art rather than to look at works of art. However useful the verbal description, analysis and interpretation, we have to experience for ourselves the implications of style, comparing and contrasting the works of different artists, schools and periods, even perhaps of different cultures.

The detail and clarity of the slides now available permit prolonged study, so that much more can be done than was at one time possible, simply by the careful selection of slides presented in such order as allows one slide to throw light upon another—a commentary in images not in words—whether the concern is with developments in a particular artist's work, with contrasts in style between say the Sienese and the Florentine school, or the meaning of one painting as against another. Many tutors still apparently feel that unless they are talking all the time they are falling down on the job, and so the visual material is never put to the fullest use, never allowed to speak for itself but drowned in a flood of talk; which does not mean to say that the tutor has only to change the slides in the projector, only that what he says should direct attention to, not distract attention from, the picture. We see only what we are looking for and the tutor has to place the students in a position where they can make their own observations, which may mean drawing their attention to certain features of pictorial representation and structure.

PRACTICAL WORK—DRAWING AND PAINTING

It was usual at one time in a programme of classes to find art under the heading "Appreciation of Art", though one looked in vain for "Appreciation of Economics", "Appreciation of Trade Unionism", or even "Appreciation of Literature". One did not, it seemed, study art but something called appreciation, which, popped on the nose like a pair of spectacles, would bring the art of any period or style into focus.

It may be simply that the term arose in distinguishing the theoretical class from the practical class in drawing and painting. These are not a university provision since, intra-murally, the study of art has been an aesthetic-historical and not a practical discipline. Perhaps in consequence of this there is a tendency, not only within university circles, to consider such classes at a lower educational level, lying in a no-man's land between craft and liberal study. Art-history has always of course enjoyed a higher intellectual status than the works of art with which it deals.

Painting is not simply a means of representing but of apprehending reality. Even where it is realised that art is something more than mimesis, that it is an expression of emotions and ideas, it is still assumed that the artist arrives at his ideas, presumably through some verbal process and then gives these pictorial form. Art is of course a language, a mode of thought as well as of communication. If the central purpose of art-education is that students shall learn this language, then it follows, since we best understand a language by using it, that the practical class is, or should be, of the greatest importance.

The exhibitions of paintings by amateur groups indicate, however, that the amateur is rarely aware that a painting is not made simply out of experience but out of a tradition. Admiring the representational skills which are a feature of our European tradition, he regards painting as representation and has no concern for its essentially formal nature. Thus a painting by Constable or Rembrandt is simply an observation of nature not an innovation upon existing traditions in landscape and portraiture. It would perhaps seem to him that Rembrandt's "Bathsheba at her Toilet" in taking the pose from a Greco-Roman bas-relief loses in originality. Painting has to assemble shapes, colours, translucencies and opacities, not only into an appearance but into a formal structure, and this we learn not from nature, not from direct experience but from art. This does not mean, of course, simply drawing upon what is given—it is reshaped by individual experience. In speaking or writing of an event we do not create a language but use the one that exists, shaping it to our needs. What we think and say, even indeed what we want to think and say, is made possible by the language in which the thought and the communication is formed.

It follows, therefore, that the painting class should not only teach the student how to handle his materials but should draw his attention to what is best and most useful to him in a long and continuing tradition. What he knows will influence what and how he paints and he will paint better for knowing Goya and Gillies than Annigoni and Russell Flint. It is particularly evident that the students in painting classes are not only ignorant of twentieth century painting but even regard it as quite simply an aberration with which they need not concern themselves. No painter is obliged to paint in the manner of Picasso, Klee, Kokoschka, Chagall, Pollock, de Stael; he is obliged; however, to be cognisant of what they have done and of its relevance to twentieth-century life. He cannot simply continue to paint as though all this rich development had never taken place.

These remarks are made not in contempt of, but with respect for, the student in practical classes. A proper development of the practical painting class is of the greatest importance to art education.

MUSIC—T. B. WILSON

> And I know not if, save in this, such gift be allowed to man,
> That out of three sounds he frame, not a fourth sound, but a star.
> (Robert Browning, *Abt Vogler*,)

Of the many qualities required of a good teacher, two stand out by virtue of their fundamental importance. First, he must have a deep knowledge and understanding of the various issues involved in his subject. Not only must he be able to command the diverse techniques and skills required by his branch of study, he must also be able to observe, penetrate, and correctly interpret what he sees, relating and integrating his findings within the framework of the subject as a whole. And yet, whatever his confidence in his skill, he must remain aware of his deficiences. He must seek constantly to extend the boundaries of his understanding, ever conscious that self-satisfaction and complacency point the way to intellectual and emotional sterility.

Secondly, he must be able to communicate his knowledge to others whose view of the subject will almost certainly differ from his own, ranging from the relatively well-informed, through the mildly inaccurate, to the wholly erroneous. He must be able to understand and even identify himself with the outlook of his students, the better to recognise the steps which must be taken to help them supplement or correct their ideas.

Both of these qualities would be generally agreed to be essential to the teaching of any subject. But both of them have perhaps a special relevance to the teaching of music, for a very large proportion of the adults who take up a study of music for the first time are beginners whose ignorance of the real nature of the subject is, in many cases, wellnigh total. In such a situation, the demands made on the student will tend to be severe, which in turn makes it vital for the tutor to possess in ample measure the combination of sound scholarship and sympathetic presentation outlined above.

Consider for a moment the enigmatic, even paradoxical aspect which music presents to such a student. He observes that it has a very real impact on him, that it possesses great power to evoke a deeply-felt response. And yet, while he may describe the experience in such terms as "gay", "sad", "pastoral" or "melancholy", he is usually aware that such descriptions are mere approximations to a much more complex and elusive plane of experience which it is beyond his power adequately to describe, and which he himself does not fully understand. He recognises that though his response may be direct and positive in character, its origins are diffuse and mysterious. On another level, the student will, under guidance, clearly perceive that music is a disciplined, precise, calculated succession of sounds—that the great composer is a "split personality" in which the artist and the craftsman are in a sense separate and yet, at the same time, indissolubly united. However, his satisfaction in this observation will be qualified by the realisation that his ability to perceive and appreciate will largely depend on the extent to which he can acquire an insight into musical procedures and techniques, and through these, the degree to which he can penetrate the labyrinthine workings of the creative mind.

Furthermore, great music abounds in apparent contradictions. For example, at first sight the music of J. S. Bach will probably appear enormously complex and diffuse, a vortex of contending sound. Yet, as Bach's work and style becomes more familiar, the impression which will grow in the student's mind will not be one of complexity but rather of directness, solidity and essential simplicity. Conversely, the elegant stability, the apparently pellucid simplicity of a Mozart will, after a time, be seen to be something of an illusion, a carapace which conceals an artistic mind which is devious and subtle in the extreme. This kind of difficulty is, of course, accentuated by the fact that music may often seem to the adult student to be the most "abstract" of the arts. It may appear to him to be remote from the externals of ordinary living, to be virtually self-sufficient, making little real contact with the outside world, or doing so only in a concealed and oblique manner. Nor is this all. Music exists in time, an intangible medium, which for study purposes is much less accommodating than, say, space. It is recorded by symbols which are in many ways inadequate to their purpose, symbols which give only a fairly close approximation to, rather than an exact representation of the music. It is perceived by the ear, an organ which is notoriously unreliable and easily misled.

In short, many adults approaching a systematic study of music for the first time find themselves confronted by very considerable difficulties to which their only real counter is an enduring and impressive enthusiasm. Even on a purely practical level, many of them are relatively poorly equipped to deal with the task they have undertaken. Often they are wholly unfamiliar with the rudiments of music. Few of them can read it with any fluency. Most of them possess only to a very limited extent the vital skill of concentrated, selective listening. In such a situation, the special relevance of the teaching qualities mentioned at the beginning is surely clear. The student's need of skilful and sympathetic guidance is acute.

At first sight, it may seem likely that such a formidable array of difficulties will so intimidate the student that he will feel unable to cope, tend to lose heart and opt for discretion rather than valour. And yet this is not the case. The reasons for this are simple. Firstly, the attraction of music is so strong and compelling for many people that their desire to increase and deepen their experience of it cannot easily be denied. Secondly, many intending students are not fully conscious of the full range of problems which confront them. Nevertheless, it is important to remember that these obstacles to progress are real and not imaginary, and that every student will sooner or later encounter them in the course of his study.

What then are the more common attitudes to music of the adult student as he prepares to embark on a serious course of study for the first time? Two main, and apparently contradictory characteristics spring to mind. The first of these is the student's sturdy independence in matters of taste. He tends, initially at least, to have fairly fixed (and often arbitrary) ideas on what he likes and dislikes, though he is usually quite open-minded on what is unknown to him, and is quite prepared to explore the unfamiliar with a view to extending the scope of his appreciative faculties. At its most severe this independence of outlook may take the form of prejudice, but this is seldom deep-rooted enough to inhibit the student's development seriously, and in most cases will yield to the gentle erosion which study provides. Indeed, this self-reliance, though it may at this stage produce erratic, inconsistent judgements, is a quality which the tutor should encourage. It is in fact one of the student's greatest assets, in that it provides a natural basis upon which he, the student, will be able to erect and develop a more reliable and informed critical faculty than that which depends on emotional reaction alone.

The second principal characteristic is one which may appear, at first sight, to be incompatible with what has been said above. And yet there can be little doubt that despite this measure of self-reliance, the adult music student almost invariably tends to be rather diffident and unassertive. He shows, in fact, all the signs of a marked inferiority complex where music is concerned, distrusting the accuracy of his judgements even as he makes them, hesitating to hazard an opinion "for fear of appearing foolish", acutely aware of his personal incompetence and inexperience. This is all the more surprising when one reflects that in such fields as politics or history or economics, the same people often express themselves volubly and even vehemently, quite undeterred by, and even failing completely to recognise, their ignorance of the issues involved. In music, on the contrary, the average student is as a rule only too conscious of his deficiences, and may even tend to magnify them out of all proportion. As the work of the class proceeds, as new and hitherto unsuspected ideas and concepts reveal themselves, musical values may seem to him to become more and more elusive and opaque in character. While the student will always have intuitively recognised that music has "meaning", it may never have occurred to him to ask what makes it meaningful. In undertaking a course of study of this type he is confronted by this very question, and finding himself on wholly unfamiliar ground quickly recognises his inability to provide the answer.

While this phase can be rather damaging to the student's self-confidence, almost invariably he will survive it without difficulty, reacting well to encouragement and guidance. Indeed, the experience is in most cases a salutary and beneficial one. It stops the student in his tracks, forcing him to think actively about things which he had in the past been content to accept passively. Where previously music may have been for him primarily an emotional experience, now his intellect, perceiving new and exciting planes of musical perspective, is no longer content to remain quiescent, but begins to play an increasingly important part in his approach to music. The object of the tutor should be to encourage this development as much as he can, his ultimate aim being to reach the stage where the student's emotional reactions are illuminated, even intensified, by his understanding, of what he hears.

The conduct of such a course of study imposes a heavy responsibility on the tutor. Success will largely depend on the degree to which he possesses the teaching qualities already discussed, and the wisdom with which he applies them to the task in hand. It will be clear from the foregoing examination of the student's frame of mind and the difficulties with which he is faced, that what he needs most at the outset is to have the basic vocabulary of music presented to him in a clear and matter-of-fact way. He must be given factual information which he himself can verify and apply under the guidance of the tutor. To counteract the student's feelings of insecurity, the tutor's initial approach should be as down-to-earth and practical as the subject will allow. The primary aim should be to communicate the basic concepts of music to the student in such a way that he can understand them intellectually and identify them aurally. For example, the student must not only know what is meant by terms like harmony and counterpoint; he must also be able to recognise them in action. He should learn, or be taught to read music, not with the painstaking exactitude which would be required of a musician, but with a general facility which will enable him to find his way about in a score. To this end, the work of the class should, whenever possible involve the use of scores. An adequate skill in score reading is not too difficult for the student to acquire, while the benefits which accrue are incalculable.

Once these conceptual and technical essentials have been made clear to the student, he should be encouraged to apply his new knowledge to actual works. He must be asked to look at music through the eyes of the composer-craftsman, observing how the profuse variety of its content is disciplined, and made to cohere and unify. He should be encouraged to get inside a work in such a way that a study of it is almost an act of re-creation. He must come to see the music as a whole conception, perceiving both the overall, large-scale pattern of the composer's thought, and the tiny details of its organisation.

While pursuing such a policy, it should always be remembered that its purpose is to further the student's appreciation and enjoyment of music. The point must never be reached where the acquisition of knowledge becomes divorced from that to which it refers. On the other hand, it must also be remembered that the one thing of which the student stands in no doubt is his emotional reactions to music. He does not need to be taught how to feel; indeed any interference in this field is presumptuous. But he does need to be shown new aspects of the subject, through which he himself can extend the boundaries of his feeling.

It may be that the impression has been given that the student is to be regarded clinically as a kind of receptacle which must be filled full of assorted information in as short a space of time as possible. One may perhaps have visions of the tutor conscientiously working his way through a long list of data, dutifully ticking each one off before moving on to the next. Obviously, the only result of such a process would be to increase the student's confusion, giving him severe mental indigestion in the process. Undeniably, if the matter is rushed through, or presented in a haphazard or pedantic way this will certainly happen. But if sympathetically handled, presented in a clear and orderly fashion and at a pace which allows the student time to absorb what he has learnt, if the process of teaching is always geared to the student's capacity to learn, and if the process of learning is supported by a sufficiency of relevant aural experience, then the student will benefit enormously. He will, in fact, become musically literate.

During this process the student will have to rely almost wholly on the guidance of the tutor. The tendency, in fact, will be for the student to accept all that the lecturer says as "ex cathedra". This is undesirable and should be continually discouraged. The whole purpose of the proposals outlined above is to increase the student's self-reliance in musical matters. The tutor should direct the student's attention patiently but insistently towards the acquisition of the basic skills of musical observation and analysis. He must constantly clarify the issues involved, encourage the student to think out problems for himself, and discourage him as much as possible from merely appropriating on trust whatever he, the tutor, may say. In short, he must give the student a foothold in the subject in order to build up his self-confidence, but he must do it in such a way that the student is required to contribute positively to the process. While the student in the early stages certainly needs guidance, understanding, and even firm direction, in the last analysis he must educate himself.

This can be a difficult, even delicate situation. The tutor is the natural leader of the class. Clearly he must play a dominant rôle in its affairs. And yet he must to some extent be self-effacing in order to allow the student to feel responsible for himself and not be completely dependent on outside help. A fine balance must be achieved in which the tutor must, as it were, supply the various premises of the syllogism while constantly encouraging the student to draw the conclusion for himself.

For the tutor who has a dynamic, out-going type of personality, this kind of self-effacement is not easy. Yet in this he must succeed. For if he fails, if he allows himself to wholly dominate the class, he will almost certainly become a kind of performer, a pied piper who by degrees mesmerises the students and himself, until the point is reached where the subject becomes secondary in importance to his presentation of it.

The first main objective then is to provide the student with the technical equipment which his course of study will require. As the student's competence increases, however, the way becomes increasingly more open to wider, more interesting and significant fields of enquiry in the pursuit of which he should be able to take a more and more active part. He will become more aware of, and interested in such considerations as style. He will begin to perceive the necessity for viewing musical developments in their historical perspective. He will begin to recognise and to enquire more actively into such matters as the relevance of music to the social conditions in which it was produced. New approaches to the subject will multiply in his mind. He will begin to see, and to understand, the vast range of expression that music embraces.

It should be understood, however, that these two stages in the student's development need not necessarily conform to any strictly chronological sequence. They are in many ways mutually complementary and can and should, where possible, be carried on simultaneously.

How far can the adult go in these studies? What difficulties or obstacles to understanding remain to be faced? Are there any perceptible limits to what he can achieve?

Quite apart from the obvious limitations imposed by the indivi-

dual's degree of aptitude and musical intelligence, there are certain
fields in which the adult's approach to music differs markedly from
that of the musician. The musician's knowledge of the subject has,
to a considerable extent, been acquired by "doing" it—for
example, his insight into harmonic subtlety or contrapuntal ingenuity is largely a consequence of the fact that he has made a
practical study of these skills. His ability to understand fully the
characteristics of a style is intensified because at some time or
another in his training he has been required to reproduce or
imitate that style. Furthermore, intensive training has increased
his aural perception of musical detail to a level much greater than
that usually possessed by the non-musician. His whole approach
to music is geared to an intimate knowledge of the skills involved
—he looks at music, as it were, from the inside.

The adult student on the other hand approaches the subject
in a quite different way. Whereas the musician is a "doer", the
adult student is an "observer"; whereas the musician is inside the
subject, the adult student tends to see it from the outside. This
does not mean that a deep knowledge and understanding of music
is beyond the adult student. On the contrary, he will usually be
able to penetrate successfully into even the most remote and
esoteric regions of the subject. But his approach to knowledge will
always and inevitably differ from that of the musician. It is of
fundamental importance that the tutor should fully recognise and
understand this difference of approach which exists between himself and his audience. Provided he does so, and adopts teaching
methods which are suitable to this situation, there are few limits
to what can be successfully attempted.

Nevertheless, there are musical regions into which the average
adult can penetrate only with difficulty. Usually this is because
an understanding of the concept or principle involved depends
largely on the kind of technical skill which is chiefly the province
of the musician. Tonality is a good example of this. Though
fundamental in importance, it is nevertheless a concept which,
despite its core of relative simplicity, is fraught with a variety of
elusive implications deriving from technical considerations of which
the non-musician knows little. In addition, an appreciation of classical tonality in its main rôle as a formal agent depends ultimately
on an aural capacity to follow its progress over extended periods of

time. Most adults find this difficult to do. And yet, so important is the principle of tonality to the music of the last 300 years, that somehow or other the student must attempt to come to grips with it. Otherwise his understanding of classical form will be hollow indeed; the diffusion and eventual dissolution of tonality which took place during the nineteenth century, and its somewhat variable rôle in the twentieth century, will be for him virtually meaningless.

As one of the aims of this volume is to be of some practical value, it might be profitable to consider at this point the ways in which a difficult idea like tonality may be communicated to an adult audience. Several possible methods suggest themselves. None of them is offered as a solution to the problem but rather as an avenue of approach through which the student may get a clearer idea of what is involved.

(1) Most adults will have a general understanding of music "being in key". What is required is that this fairly amorphous reaction should be sharpened up and the student's attention directed to the other important attributes of tonality. For example, he should be encouraged to see it on the one hand as a source of colour in music, and, on the other hand as an organising principle of the greatest importance, a kind of musical "force of gravity" which helps to discipline music and impart to it a sense of direction and purpose.

(2) Still on a general level, most students have a tonal sense which, though very strong and deep-rooted, is almost completely passive. To help stimulate this tonal instinct into activity, a useful device is to confront the student with a piece of music in which the tonal element is quite blatantly defective. This can be done by improvising a short diatonic passage which ends say on the subdominant rather than on the expected tonic level. Most people perceive clearly that such a passage is unsatisfactory, and this in turn helps them to a greater awareness of the powerful influence which tonality exerts in music. However, while this device often provides a useful stimulant and makes the student aware of the importance of tonality, it is, as an approach, essentially negative, and its usefulness is therefore limited.

(3) A more positive line is to choose for study and intensive listening a work, or part of a work, in which clearly-defined tonalities succeed one another in close succession. A good example

of this is to be found in the 2nd movement of Bach's Concerto in
D Minor for two violins and strings. The tonal range used to display
the principal melody is quite wide, and the various "blocks" of
tonality are quite clearly differentiated from one another. Such
an example provides the student with a clear, simple instance of
one of the ways in which tonality may be used. Even better suited
to the purpose of such study, perhaps, are fugato passages and
fugal expositions, for these give the student the opportunity of
establishing in his mind the all-important relationship between
the tonic and dominant keys which is so fundamental to the
musical thinking of the past. However, examples should be chosen
with some care. Most suitable are those which preserve a degree
of directness and simplicity—that is, those in which the idiom and
the texture are relatively uncomplicated—examples, in fact, in
which the student will be less distracted by the actual material
and more able to concentrate on the tonal sequence of events.
Unfortunately, much fugal writing is not particularly accommodating in this respect. It might therefore be a good idea to begin on a
"do-it-yourself" level by constructing examples of one's own, using
perhaps well-known tunes like "Au Clair de la Lune" as "subjects".
Thereafter one can proceed to more orthodox examples selected
from the vast literature available.

(4) Another approach is to promote in the student a greater
awareness of modulation. Obviously, abrupt and colourful modulations will be the easiest ones to detect, whereas the more gradual
and imperceptible types may present greater difficulty. The
complete process of modulation may be, and often is, lengthy,
involving as it does the destruction of the old key and the estab-
lishment of the new. But if the student can be taught to recognise
the vital point at which the equilibrium of the old key is first
disturbed, then he should be able to follow the remainder of the
process with some success, and in so doing achieve a certain
amount of insight into this important aspect of tonal procedure.
The degree of this success will depend to a large extent upon the
nature of the style involved. While it is impossible to generalise
about this, one might as a rule expect that modulations occurring
in the predominantly diatonic language of Haydn or Mozart
would be fairly readily perceptible, in that the shift of tonal
emphasis, though seldom dramatic and often subtle, is nevertheless

usually made quite clear. In a more elaborate or chromatic idiom, however, tonal outlines are often less clearly defined, and may appear to the student to be somewhat blurred and opaque. As a result, modulations taking place in this kind of context will often be more difficult to follow.

It must be remembered that a thorough understanding of all the aspects and implications of tonality depends ultimately upon possession of the musical skills mentioned earlier. It may be that the purposes of the course of study being followed will require the tutor to embark on a study of elementary harmony with his class, and there is little doubt that a greater degree of success will be obtained if this is done. But even without this, an approach such as the one outlined above will usually succeed in making the student actively aware of the nature and function of tonality, though his ability to follow its progress with precision may remain limited.

This, of course, is but one example of the type of problem in communication which confronts the tutor. Others are not hard to find. One need look no further than the music of the present day to find a subject which calls in full for the qualities of sound scholarship and sympathetic presentation which were emphasised at the outset. A great deal of relevant comment on these problems and many important considerations have here only been hinted at or presented in the merest outline. What has been made clear and insisted upon is that the primary objective of adult education in music is to encourage the student to develop within himself a sound and confident critical faculty, fostering his enthusiasm and extending as far as possible the boundaries of his musical experience and understanding. It cannot be sufficiently stressed, however, that the attention to detail which is a necessary part of this development should never be allowed to obscure the main issue, nor become an end in itself. For knowledge, and the increased perception which it brings, should be cultivated only as means whereby the student can transcend detail, see the subject in its wider aspect, and achieve a degree of appreciation and enjoyment greater than that which he previously possessed. The wonder of music will remain, for ultimately it is beyond our understanding. But it is important that our sense of awe should proceed, as it does in Browning's *Abt Vogler*, from informed insight rather than from ignorance.

CHAPTER IX

SCIENCE

William C. Hutchison

SCIENCE is no newcomer to the adult education scene. Much has been written elsewhere[1] on the science teaching in the Mechanics' Institutes and on the Extension Courses arranged by the Universities of Cambridge, Oxford and London at the end of the last century. The beginning of the twentieth century saw a great demand for such subjects as economics, history, and politics stimulated to a large extent by the growth of the Workers' Educational Association. Science thus temporarily lost its position of popularity as a subject for adult classes, but only temporarily since this period of declining interest in the field of adult education was one of great activity in the field of scientific research. The foundations laid in the previous century were ready to build upon, and hardly a branch of science has not witnessed spectacular developments and advances during the first half of this century. These advances and discoveries have not only changed the face of science but have affected dramatically the lives of all of us. It is not surprising, therefore, that the adult education movement which must always be alive to current thought and activity, has reawakened its interest in the teaching of science.

It is not proposed to discuss here at length whether science is a "suitable" subject for inclusion in adult education provision. A great deal has been written about the liberalising influence of science and its value as a humane study. There is no doubt about the value of science in disciplining and training the mind. It cultivates objective observation and trains the student in logical reasoning and in independent judgement. It inculcates a healthy scepticism towards any attempt at dogmatism and, above all, it appeals to that most fundamental characteristic of the human mind, curiosity.[2]

Such considerations would make it easy to justify the teaching of science in the realm of adult education, but perhaps the simplest reason and, at the present time, one of the most cogent, is the tremendous interest in science which exists outside the ranks of the professional scientists. It is necessary, therefore, that the scientist should add to his duties of advancing knowledge and training future scientists, that of satisfying the public demand for information about science.

What does the public want? In the provision of classes in the various scientific disciplines, there is considerable variation in demand. It is true, however, that in general the public want instruction in "straight" science—clear, factual accounts of what science has to say about the nature of the universe and of this world in particular. Attempts to discuss scientific method in an abstract way or to hang science on to a sociological peg are, except in special cases, unlikely to be successful.

It is at the same time broadly true that the demand for factual information cannot be met by a popular lecture of the type common in the latter part of the nineteenth century. There may be a place for such a didactic presentation in the medium of television, but the average mature adult will want to question statements, to demand further evidence and amplification, and to discuss the implications of particular scientific discoveries. This means that the formal lecture is unsuited to adult needs and the tutorial type of class, modified to suit the requirements of the subject, is often a more satisfactory technique.

Nevertheless, in the presentation of science to adults there is frequently a very proper need for the tutor to spend time on exposition. Even though with the increasing amount of science taught at school and with more scientific programmes on radio and television, more members of an adult class may be expected to have some acquaintance with the rudiments of the subject, it is still true that, except with special groups, the tutor must spend time in straightforward factual instruction. The important point is that the lecture must be of the right type.[3]

Many science classes for adults are taken by members of the internal science departments of our universities to whom, particularly at the outset of their academic career, the formal lecture seems the simplest and most obvious of teaching methods. This is the method by which they themselves have been instructed and by which they are accustomed to instruct undergraduates.

Frequently they fail to appreciate that the approach to an adult audience has to be very carefully thought out. With university undergraduates, whose attendance at a course of lectures is obligatory, it is normal practice to develop the subject logically and systematically, ensuring that elementary theory is firmly implanted before advanced ideas are mentioned. For the adult group, whose attendance is voluntary, such an approach is doomed to failure. A good lecture to such a group is not a cut-and-dried delivery from a set of notes but is a statement of a particular subject carefully adapted to the audience of the evening. The method of presentation will depend on the nature of the audience, on what the tutor has been able to discover of their background and interests. Frequently it will be necessary to "put the cart before the horse" and introduce an advanced idea followed by the elucidation of the elementary theory on which it is based. This development of the subject may well be achieved by discussion in which the members of the group participate.

It is important, therefore, that the tutor should be prepared to rethink his whole subject before attempting to present it to an adult class. He must be prepared to organise the approach to his material to cater for what he assumes to be the interests of the class, and he must modify and adapt when he discovers what these interests really are—a discovery which cannot be made until after he meets the class. Thought must also be given to the preparation of the discussion. With some groups and with some subjects, good discussion can perhaps be relied on to arise spontaneously, but in general the tutor will have to spend some time framing suitable questions and ideas for consideration by the class. This is perhaps especially important in some branches of science where the individual members of the class may not have much personal experience on which to draw.[4]

These are some of the specific points which are of importance in the general presentation of science in adult education. But one quality of the tutor which overrides, and indeed includes, all that has been said is an enthusiasm for his subject. A good university degree and professional competence are necessary if proper educational standards are to be maintained, but these in themselves are of little consequence if the tutor is not enthusiastic about his subject and about the idea of getting it across to his class.

Given this, the problems of presentation will tend to solve themselves and the initial difficulties will be overcome, for the enthusiast will always adapt and modify his methods if they do not produce the best results.

At this stage, some consideration might be given to the question of whether the organisation of science classes for adults should be in the hands of a professional scientist, that is to say, in the context of the university extra-mural department, a full-time staff tutor in science. There is no doubt that where no such appointment exists substantial developments in the provision of science classes can still be made. In so far as the job of the organiser is to arrange for particular demands to be met, reasonable co-operation on the part of the members of internal science departments will ensure that some of these will be satisfied.

The scope and interest of the programme will, however, be readily enlarged if a full-time appointment of a scientist is made. Scientists are in short supply but their use in this way can be justified if one studies the statistics of class provision and attendance in those universities whose extra-mural departments include staff tutors in science. The full-time tutor can suggest topics for study and can assess the merit and suitability of courses offered by his colleagues. Perhaps most important of all, he is the channel of communication between the world of adult education and the scientific community. He learns of opportunities for co-operation with scientific societies and his contacts with his scientific colleagues in internal departments are such that the job of finding part-time tutors with the right qualifications and temperament is considerably eased. When it comes to advising a new tutor (or even an old-established one !) how best to present his subject to a particular audience or to selecting aspects most suitable for adult education, such advice is the more acceptable when offered by a fellow scientist. In the reverse direction, the full-time science tutor can help to make out a case for the various "aids" which part-time tutors require for teaching different aspects of science.

In the budget of any university the expenditure on the teaching of science is high because of the cost of running practical classes and the necessity, for modern research, of providing costly apparatus. Moreover, scientific knowledge has been acquired by the experimental approach, and it is not therefore surprising to find that many hold the view that in the field of adult education the provision of science classes must also be a costly business with the provision of laboratory facilities a necessity. Certainly a class in which the students *do* something is better than one in which they listen passively to the tutor, but what they do is perhaps of secondary importance. Student participation may not necessarily mean laboratory or field work; in some cases an assessment of the evidence for some particular speculation may be a useful way of training in logical deduction. Nevertheless, there is much to be said for demonstration experiments and if in addition facilities exist for some experiments to be carried out by the members of the class themselves the advantages are great. The difficulty in obtaining the desired result, and the reasons for failure in themselves offer opportunity for class discussion.[5]

In most sciences, simple experiments can be devised which illustrate the difficulties of precise measurement and a study of the collected results of the class may afford suitable material for a discussion of experimental error and possibly for an introduction to statistical analysis. Within a university centre, of course, laboratory facilities and apparatus are usually readily available and much can be done by the tutor in providing demonstration experiments. How far, under these circumstances, the students themselves carry out experimental work depends on the nature of the subject of study and on the composition of the group. In some subjects, such as observational astronomy or botany, there would appear to be no arguments against student practical work provided facilities exist, whereas in others, such as chemistry or bacteriology, the tutor must decide from his knowledge of the members of the group, whether class experiments may safely be carried out.

Outside the university centre itself, lack of modern equipment need not preclude experimental demonstrations or even a programme of class experiments. A little thought will often enable a scientific principle to be demonstrated satisfactorily using very simple apparatus. After all, many of the fundamental discoveries in science were made without the paraphernalia of the modern research laboratory. Indeed, experiments carried out with simple apparatus often illustrate the point more clearly than those involving complex equipment, and there is much to be said for

keeping this in mind even when full resources are available. Some
tutors have found it useful to assemble a collection of simple
demonstration equipment and specimens which can be packed for
easy transport to outlying centres and which can be rapidly set
up when required.

Where no apparatus is available, and even when it is, visual
aids are of great usefulness. In science teaching, perhaps the most
important of these are the lantern slide and its variant, the film
strip. Slides, especially the 2 $\times$ 2 in. size, are easily transportable,
and a projector for the size mentioned is nowadays a fairly common piece of equipment in schools, halls and in many homes.
Coloured slides, particularly, may be used to great advantage to
show, for example, botanical and zoological specimens in their
natural habitats at different seasons of the year, geologically
important sites and samples of rocks and minerals. In physiology
and biochemistry classes, too, slides offer the possibility of showing
a class selected pictures of the effects of hormone imbalance or
vitamin deficiencies, to name but two topics. Similarly, in other
scientific disciplines the slide has its special function.

In short, the slide enables the tutor to show to his class material
which it would be impracticable to show in actuality. It can,
therefore, be thought of as a special form of scientific demonstration.

Closely allied to the slide in function is the film. There has
been much interest in recent years in scientific films and there is
now available, in the popular 16 mm size, a very wide range of
films covering most aspects of scientific study. It must, however,
be admitted that there are difficulties. In the first place the equipment for projection is much more costly and therefore less readily
available outside the main towns and cities. Ciné projectors may,
of course, be hired but transportation to distant centres, unless
the tutor travels by car, may be a difficulty.

Secondly, films are expensive to make and few, if any, organisations concerned with adult education are likely to be able to
afford to purchase copies of all the films which they would like
to use for teaching purposes. Although a number of films are
available on free loan, recourse must usually be had to hiring from
commercial film libraries. Not only is this liable to constitute a
major item of expenditure in the budget for a class, but also it

necessitates booking the film for a particular date well in advance. This in turn restricts the tutor in his approach to the subject since he must reach a particular point by a certain evening, otherwise the showing of the film has no relevance. It would be better to allow the development of the subject to proceed at a pace suited to the classes and along the lines suggested by the discussion, making the decision to show the film only when the classes have, on their own, reached a stage when they will profit by seeing it. Unfortunately, the number of demands for bookings with which the film libraries have to cope, renders such an educationally satisfactory method quite impracticable.

Finally, there is the quality of the film itself. As has been said, there is now available a very wide selection of scientific films, but not all are of equal merit and not all are suitable for the purposes of adult education. Film catalogues do give some information about the content of a film and the type of audience for which it is suited, but the compilers of the catalogues do not have a particular adult class or the approach of a particular tutor in mind, and it often happens that the film, when it arrives, turns out to be unsuitable. It may be too advanced or too elementary; it may spend a lot of time dealing with topics already adequately covered by the class, or it may give scant attention to the point which the tutor hoped would be developed in detail. There is no easy answer to this difficulty. It is obviously impracticable to spend time and money previewing all the films available on a particular subject. The average tutor operating under the usual conditions will probably find it technically difficult to show a class a series of short excerpts from a number of films—as has been done, for example, very successfully in a number of scientific television programmes. The only solution, therefore, is to learn the hard way, keeping careful notes of the suitability or otherwise of the films borrowed from the film libraries and making use of opinions offered by colleagues and in the review sections of periodicals such as *Discovery*. In this way, over a few years, the tutor should have little difficulty in building up a selection of film titles which he knows to be suitable adjuncts to his own teaching methods and to his own approach to his subject.

The films available vary very much in their technique. Some may be purely pictorial, showing different types of landscape and geological formation or studying living creatures in their natural environment; a number of recent films dealing with the life histories of small animals are quite fascinating, and afford a way of showing a class something which, in the normal course of events, they could never study at first hand.

Other films show various aspects of the application of scientific knowledge. These may deal with industrial processes in the chemical industry, in the preparation and processing of food, or in the production and testing of drugs. In some cases it may be possible for the class to visit industrial concerns and see for themselves something of the scientific processes involved. But where this is not possible the film forms a very useful substitute. Many of the films in this category are produced and distributed (usually free) by the industrial firms themselves, e.g. Imperial Chemical Industries Ltd., Shell Petroleum Products, and Unilever, and though most, understandably, incorporate a certain amount of advertisement for particular products of the firm concerned, this rarely interferes with their educational value.

Still other films are concerned with the presentation of the fundamental facts of pure science. Many of these incorporate demonstration experiments, including some of great historical interest, which it would otherwise be impossible to show to the class. These films and others often use the animated cartoon principle to build up moving diagrams which are useful for conveying a visual impression of, for example, cyclic processes in a way which could never be achieved with a static picture.

Films can be obtained covering both elementary and advanced topics, suitable for general and specialised audiences. It is worth noting that, in addition to the catalogues issued by the commercial film libraries and industrial firms, lists of films covering the various aspects of particular scientific subjects are issued by certain learned societies and professional bodies, e.g. the Physiological Society and the Royal Institute of Chemistry.

Many of the films available are excellent aids to the teaching of science to adults, but it must be emphasised that they should never be regarded as anything other than aids. Most classes welcome films which are often entertaining as well as being instructive and the temptation sometimes arises to substitute a film for personal instruction by the tutor. This should be resisted.

In general it is preferable to use a film to supplement or re-capitulate an argument already developed by class discussion, though sometimes the film may form the starting point of discussion.

Another form of visual aid which some science tutors like to use is the wall chart. This has the advantage over the slide that one or more charts can be displayed at the same time and indeed may be kept up throughout the class period for reference as occasion demands. If small copies of the charts can be duplicated for distribution to the students for private study, the value of this method of teaching is greatly enhanced. Wall charts should, of course, be kept simple and not encumbered with detail.

Even the simplest chart, however, presents a complete picture. The student is confronted with the end of the argument at the same time as he sees the beginning of it. For this reason, some tutors prefer to develop the material suitable for a wall chart step by step on the blackboard. There is much to commend this practice. Moreover, the student is encouraged to construct in his notebook his own diagrams logically and step by step, a process which is much better from the educational point of view than copying down a completed diagram displayed as a small chart.

A complete discussion of teaching aids in science teaching for adults should include a number of special pieces of equipment which are useful for instruction in certain science subjects. For example, a cathode ray oscilloscope is useful for physics and physiology, not to mention electronics and electrical engineering. Microscopes are an obvious accessory for certain subjects, while a tape recorder has its uses in physiology to demonstrate heart sounds and for other purposes. Some of these special requirements will be considered under the appropriate subject heading, for it is necessary to consider which branches of science are best suited for study in adult education and how these may best be presented.

It is sometimes regretted that scientists today are so highly specialised that many are unable to present their subjects with the breadth of approach which is desirable for many adult classes. There are certainly few scientists today who would profess an up-to-date acquaintance with the details of several unrelated scientific disciplines. Most science tutors would perhaps like to restrict themselves to the particular field of knowledge in which

F

they can justifiably profess competence, but discussion in adult classes has an unnerving knack at times of moving suddenly into some related but, to the tutor, somewhat foreign field. This is not to be resisted overmuch, for scientific knowledge is an integral whole and the subdivisions into different disciplines are, to some extent, artificial. Most classes will respect the tutor who admits that he does not know the answer to a question outside his own experience and will be happy to join with him in trying to ferret out information from other sources. To some extent this inability of adult education to stick to the traditional type of syllabus for academic and professional courses helps to make it challenging and stimulating for the tutor. Nevertheless, lack of a detailed knowledge of scientific disciplines other than one's own can some-times be a handicap, and in the present context it is difficult for the writer with a training in biochemistry to be familiar with all the problems which may arise in teaching the various sciences. If some subjects seem therefore to be treated in greater detail than others, this is the reason.

Astronomy[6] has a long-established history as a subject for adult classes and the present classes in this subject are in general thriving and successful. They fall broadly speaking into four groups. The first group consists of elementary classes in general astronomy which cater for those who have an interest in what they see in the sky at night or who have read some popular articles on the subject and want to find out more. The second group are really classes in physics with an astronomical bias. The third and fourth groups are more advanced and deal respectively with mathematical aspects of astronomy and with cosmological theory. In this age of rockets, satellites, and manned space craft there are obviously problems of space research which can be discussed under any of the four groups mentioned.

Where observatory facilities exist, classes in general astronomy would be expected to make some use of a telescope. This is useful and obvious practical work, but students must be taught first of all what to look for and why, otherwise the use of the telescope becomes mere gadgetry. Considerations of angles and of relative motions of planets and stars lead to an appreciation of size and distance. Even with no telescope much can usefully be taught. Sooner or later, however, various physical ideas have to be explained and many courses are really courses in physics which start from an initial interest in astronomy. Optics, atomic and nuclear physics, radiation, spectra, gravitation, the Doppler effect, and many other topics can all be studied in a course entitled "Astronomy".

A great deal can be done with only a limited use of mathematics. A statement of the assumptions made and the conclusions reached using mathematics will often be acceptable without detailing the steps involved in the calculation. Nevertheless, a proportion of students may be expected to have the training and the desire to investigate further and, for such, a more advanced mathematical treatment may be profitable. Cosmological questions, too, are bound to occur in general courses and current interest in such ideas is not inconsiderable, due in some measure to the writings and broadcast talks of Hoyle and others. For the more advanced student a course on cosmology is a definite possibility.[7]

Physics courses as such may also be varied in their approach.[8] Some tutors confine their attention to classical physics and deal with mechanics and hydrostatics, heat, light, sound, and electricity. Such an approach can impart a large amount of very useful information. Many of the relevant facts can be demonstrated with the simplest of apparatus, and the topics mentioned provide admirable illustrations of logical scientific deduction. To the general public, however, classical physics is not so exciting as present day developments in the subject, so one finds classes in atomic and nuclear physics attracting greater numbers.[9] Such classes may cater for the general public, but there is also a need for special classes for physics graduates who find that their subject has changed so rapidly that their knowledge is no longer up-to-date. Schoolteachers of physics may well find themselves in this position.

Although "straight" classical physics may not attract a large following when offered as a subject for adult study, it is frequently possible to approach it from the standpoint of some special interest or hobby. Thus, an interest in music could lead to a study of sound and acoustics, while a scientific study of photography would include, among other topics, the study of optics.

In producing a syllabus for a class in physics—and, indeed, in any science—what should be emphasised is not a massive collection of facts. Certain main principles should be stressed to show their fundamental clarity and simplicity. Physics is a valuable study for demonstrating what is implicit in scientific method; it illustrates perhaps better than any other science the application of the principle of causality to a wide range of phenomena. Adult students may not acquire much in the way of factual knowledge, which is all too rapidly forgotten, but if, after being members of a class in physics, they have learned something of the logic of scientific method, and can detect fallacious reasoning, then, from an educational point of view, the operation is surely justified.

In the realm of Applied Physics and Engineering not a great deal has been attempted. There is probably scope for classes for specialised groups in the various branches of engineering who wish to keep pace with modern developments. Classes may also be run in electronics for those whose jobs involve the use of electronic equipment, such as some medical research workers. This subject also offers the possibility of a more general course, since electronic devices are now familiar features of our daily lives, and the "How does it work?" spirit of curiosity can be followed up. Care must be taken, however, that such a course does not develop into an exhibition of gadgetry and the basic scientific principles lost sight of.

Mathematics classes in adult education provision tend to be rather specialised, and to cater only for those who have a reasonable preliminary knowledge of the subject. Some classes are devoted to a study of the philosophy and logic of mathematics, while others deal with particular mathematical topics. Statistics is a fairly popular choice, and is liable to attract a number of students who already have a training in other scientific disciplines. The current interest in satellites may also be used to encourage the study of geometry and dynamics.

Like physics, mathematics has undergone marked changes in recent years and there is therefore a place for refresher courses for mathematics graduates to bring their understanding of the subject up to date. Classes may be arranged, for example, on the theory of sets or on various aspects of the axiomatic structure characteristic of twentieth century mathematics.

The introduction of digital computers into business and research has been followed by a demand for courses on these machines. What can be done to meet this demand depends on the type of computer which is available for illustrative purposes and for class use. Special courses can be devoted to the use of computers in various fields.

Chemistry is a subject which has never figured prominently in adult education programmes. This is perhaps primarily due to a feeling that chemical formulae and equations cannot be coped with by the average adult class and secondarily to a somewhat unjustified association of practical chemistry with "stinks" and "bangs". Neither of these objections will really stand close examination. If the tutor is prepared to think out suitable approaches to the subject and introduce the class gently to the idea of formulae as a convenient pictorial representation of the substances of which all things are composed, he will be rewarded by as great an expression of interest in this method of looking at the world around us as in any other. There are many points of interest which, for different groups, can form a suitable starting point— minerals, crystals, metals, explosives, plastics, and a variety of domestic commodities. Food and the composition of the human body is also a clear line of approach, and, though this may be thought of in academic terms as more appropriately classified under biochemistry, adult education rightly does not have to recognise hard and fast boundaries between different scientific disciplines.

The question of practical work need not be a difficulty. Once again much can be achieved with the minimum of apparatus and reagents and, if full laboratory facilities are available, the range of demonstration experiments which can be carried out is extensive. Nevertheless, many of the reagents used are corrosive and some may be dangerous if not handled correctly, so the tutor must judge beforehand the competence of the class to carry out experiments on their own. In any case he would be well advised to check on the insurance cover against possible accident ! A useful form of practical activity by chemistry classes consists of works visits to study the industrial applications of chemical processes.

The science of geology[10] has always been popular as a subject for adult education classes and it has a number of obvious advantages. In the first place it caters quite obviously for the interest which undoubtedly exists in the countryside and the things which can be seen there. The students come with a stock of experiences and observations of the weather, scenery, rocks and building stones of their own locality and of others visited, perhaps on holiday. Specimens collected by the class may be examined and, in a sense, the surrounding district becomes the laboratory. The information collected should be amplified by the tutor who may be able to draw on a wide range of specimens of rocks, minerals and fossils from the local university geology department or perhaps from a local museum.[11] The students can be encouraged to draw the specimens and to compare different ones. This will produce questions and from the answers suitable material for discussion may arise. Facilities for preparing specimens for microscopic examination obviously extend the scope of study, but a great deal may be achieved without such aids.

Such examination of specimens is very necessary, but an important aspect of geology from the standpoint of adult education is the study of rocks in the mass and the evolution of the landscape. In this connexion, class excursions are of paramount importance and the geology tutor has this advantage over his colleagues in botany and zoology, that his field study material is always in exactly the same position on each occasion. What can be achieved by excursions depends, of course, on such factors as the size of the class and the geological resources of the locality. But there must be few areas which cannot produce some useful material for field work. Many individual students may be stimulated sufficiently to engage in solitary field studies and discussion of their observations, or examination of specimens collected by them can constitute a useful part of the class activity.

Excursions to all sites of geological interest are impracticable and lantern slides are of great use in illustrating the larger features of scenery. Ideally, these should be studied and discussed by the class and not merely used as illustrations. In this way students will be trained in observation and will begin to notice features in the landscape and evidences of geological processes which would otherwise escape them.

Another interesting avenue of approach to the study of geology is by way of palaeontology. This, of course, brings in evolution and forms a linking point with the biological sciences. The concept of geological time is of vital importance for a proper appreciation of evolution.

From introductory studies of specimens of rocks, minerals, and fossils and consideration of the forces which have shaped the landscape, more advanced classes can proceed to a more formal and systematic study of the broader principles of geology. The study and interpretation of geological maps would form a logical part of the syllabus for such courses, and a stock of such maps would be a useful purchase if much teaching of geology is contemplated.

Biological studies are, in general, popular with adults. Courses giving a bird's eye view of the various forms of living things may form useful introductions to biology for there is a genuine interest in the other living creatures which populate the earth. For such courses no special degree of technical skill is required on the part of the student and local interest can often be maintained by using the plants and animals of the area as subjects for study. Unfortunately, all the material desired is not available at all seasons of the year and it is common for classes in botany and zoology to extend into the spring and summer months when profitable excursions may be undertaken. Not that the winter months should be regarded as useless from this point of view but, in general, more abundant material for study can be obtained at other seasons.

Biology courses may take many forms.[12] Botany classes may devote themselves to a systematic study of form and function in the plant with extensive use of floras. Such studies have often been followed by useful field work in which the class undertake a survey of the plant life of an area and compile a regional flora. This is an ideal field of endeavour for the trained amateur, and since the distribution of plants is liable to change, there is no harm in surveying the same region many times. For such work the tutor collates and interprets the results and acts as adviser. Other botany classes may study problems of plant ecology or may relate botanical knowledge to such fields as forestry, agriculture and horticulture.

Adult studies in zoology tend to follow a similar sort of pattern. There are the systematic studies of the diversity of animal life, and the courses dealing with particular groups of animals. The latter may be restricted to animals found in a particular environment as in various courses in marine biology or they may deal with a specialised type of adaptation, as in courses on parasitology. One popular topic is ornithology but it must be admitted that

many who come to the classes in this subject are interested merely
in species identification. If ornithology is to be justified as suitable
for inclusion in a programme of scientific studies for adults, it is
important that the tutor should endeavour to take the class beyond
this stage and consider the basic scientific problems of bird biology
—problems such as behaviour and display, breeding cycles, and
migration.

Evolution is a topic which arouses interest, but it is doubtful
whether courses should be devoted exclusively to this topic. It
should, however, be included in the great majority of biology
courses, where most tutors will find that it arises, quite logically,
in the course of discussion. A comprehensive treatment of the
subject demands acquaintance with many of the sciences and the
tutor may have to spend a considerable amount of time filling in
the background necessary for a full discussion of all the evidence
for the occurrence of evolution, and still more time for a discussion
of the possible ways in which it might have occurred.

Practical work in zoology depends very much on the aspect of
the subject chosen. Ornithology and marine biology classes will
obviously benefit by excursions to study the subject in the field.
Simple dissection can be carried out with the minimum of apparatus. For other topics a microsocpe will be necessary. As in
botany there is scope for valuable field work by the trained
amateur. This is perhaps well accepted in the case of birds, but
with other species useful observations can be made of behaviour
and distribution. There are a number of adult education classes
in biology which have contributed material to scientific journals,
and the methods used to carry out the observations often show
great ingenuity.

In geology, botany and zoology co-operation with local scientific
societies and museums is often of considerable benefit. The former
may afford an opportunity for the presentation of the results of
investigations carried out by members of the class and the members
of the society will frequently welcome opportunities for more
intensive scientific study during the winter months.

The study of biology includes the study of the human species.
A course of wide interest can be organised to cover various aspects
of the structure and function of the human body, physical anthropology,[13] human genetics, and human evolution. Such a course

can profitably extend over three or four years, and has evident links with sociological studies.

Biology courses, which study the economy of nature, the way in which plants and animals affect one another and how their populations are controlled in nature, lead naturally to a discussion of how the principles of natural control have been exploited by man in the development of biological control methods as practised against certain pests of agriculture and forestry. Such a study can be extended to include the general questions of man's rôle in altering the landscape and his future in relation to food production and the expanding world population.

Adult interest in biology being undoubtedly due to the fact that man himself is part of the world of living things, it is not surprising to find a demand for courses dealing with the human body itself in health and disease. General courses in physiology approaching the subject from the standpoint of the function of the major systems of the body, or courses in anatomy which start from the structure of the body, provide useful introductions. Students can learn a great deal from observation of their own and other people's bodies. If the tutor can introduce comparative anatomy and physiology to his class a great deal of useful scientific information can be taught.

The study of the physiological functions of the body leads quite naturally to an interest in other fields. Disordered conditions of the body can be treated by various drugs, so courses in pharmacology are called for and these give an opportunity to discuss the wide range of pharmaceutical substances in use today. An interest in disease means an interest in the agents causing disease, and from this develop courses in bacteriology and virology; and it is not a difficult task to extend the interest from pathogenic bacteria to the non-pathogens.

At a somewhat more specialised level than that of general physiology a study can be made of biochemistry. As with chemistry itself this subject has often been avoided on the ground that it is too difficult for the average adult group. Certainly only a specialised group will be able to cope with, for example, advanced enzyme kinetics or a detailed study of the energy relationships of the various reactions occurring in the living cell. But there is much which is fascinating and readily understandable by an average

adult group. Many of the biological topics which have already
been mentioned as points of interest have a chemical basis and
these can form a useful starting point for discussion.

One fairly obvious avenue of approach is the nutritional. A
consideration of the chemical nature of the body and of the food
consumed leads to a discussion of the nature of digestion with a
brief look at the properties and function of enzymes *en passant*.
It is not necessary at this stage to discuss the detailed chemistry
of the substances involved. The idea that proteins and carbo-
hydrates are complex substances made up of simple units known
respectively as amino acids and sugars is quite adequate. Later,
when intermediary metabolism is covered, some more detail of
chemical structure may be required, but by this stage the class
should be ready to accept it. Minerals and vitamins are introduced
at appropriate points in the course and the question of control
and co-ordination of the body activities leads to a study of hor-
mones and, if desired, the biochemistry of nervous tissue. Later,
the course may be given a special slant according to the needs or
wishes of the class. Nutrition may be studied in greater depth,
pathological conditions and the use of biochemistry in the diag-
nosis and treatment of disease discussed, or consideration given
to comparative aspects of non-mammalian biochemistry.

Another topical course in this field can link biochemistry with
the science of genetics, the study of which has been well established
with adult classes. Man is looked at, not from the point of view of
the general pattern of chemical activity in his body, but from the
angle of individual chemical differences. The classical examples of
inborn errors of metabolism and of blood groups have an obvious
link with heredity. Mendelian inheritance is discussed and a study
of the cytological features of mitosis and meiosis leads on to a
consideration of the chemical nature of the genetic material.
There is no need to discuss the chemical structure of nucleic acids
in great detail but it is perfectly possible to implant the idea that
the order of bases in DNA spells out a code word which the cell
can interpret and also that the double stranded structure (which
does not require to be helical for the purposes of our argument)
allows the possibility of molecular replication. The part played by
RNA in protein synthesis can be outlined, and the recent work
in this field on "breaking the genetic code" opens up an exciting

prospect. The action of bacteriophage and the transforming principle in bacteria all contribute to building up a picture which cannot fail to fascinate any thinking group of adults.

For special groups there are many other medical and veterinary subjects which can form suitable topics for study, but of these, few are suited to the general adult audience.

Geography is sometimes thought of as on the borders of science, and some aspects of it may appropriately be considered in this chapter. Meteorology, involving the scientific study of the weather, is a topic of great interest, certainly to inhabitants of the British Isles, and when the geographer takes the synoptic view of geology, meteorology and human ecology, he indulges in a scientific study which can be linked immediately to many social problems.

In the early days of reawakened interest in science in adult education, many pleas were made for the study of the history and philosophy of science.[14] In the context of economic and sociological studies which had developed after the turn of the century, such views are perhaps not surprising. Nevertheless, present experience suggests that such courses will not attract good classes, though adults who have already attended a number of classes on scientific subjects may profit by them. At the same time, the historical view of the development of a particular science usually results in its being studied in the logical order and a useful course can be built around the historical approach, provided that a large proportion of the time is devoted to looking in detail at particular scientific discoveries and the experimental evidence on which they are based.

Courses in subjects which to some extent cut across the conventional barriers between different sciences have much to commend them in the field of adult education. Obvious examples are astrophysics, geochemistry and cell biology. Radioisotopes, too, lend themselves to a discussion of elementary atomic physics coupled with a study of their uses in various fields—medical, biological, agricultural or industrial. Some modern scientific developments may make it profitable to re-examine the relations between science and religion.

In all science courses two ever-present problems are the choice of title to be used and the extent of the technical vocabulary which has to be employed. In general, the title must have some meaning for the prospective student. The names of some sciences, such as astronomy and botany, are well known and understood and courses may be so entitled. The student will be confident that he knows something of what the course is to be about, though the tutor may show him aspects of the subject the existence of which he never suspected. Other sciences may be more esoteric or may have an unjustified association with complexity and difficulty, and in such cases the tutor would be well advised to popularise his title though there is a danger that too "clever" a title may fail to convey the true content of the course and so attract the wrong type of audience.

Technical terms cannot, of course, be avoided in science teaching. But the tutor will do well to examine carefully those that he proposes to use and exclude those for which ordinary language can easily be substituted. There are, unfortunately, many examples in science of terms which have been coined and which then convey an impression that a particular phenomenon is understood whereas they are really a cloak for ignorance. Such jargon should be avoided—not only in adult education—and use made only of terms which give succinct expression to an idea which would otherwise require a long explanation.

It is difficult in the space of this chapter to give much detailed advice on the question of suitable books for adult classes in science.[15] Certainly, in some fields there is still a dearth of books suitable for this type of student, though the situation has greatly improved from what it was some years ago. Particular mention should be made of the series of Pelican Books published by Penguin Books Ltd. Many of these are admirable, up-to-date accounts of modern scientific knowledge written in relatively simple language and available at a reasonable price. Though more expensive, the New Naturalist series published by Collins will be found of great use in many adult classes, while another useful modern series in biology is published by Prentice-Hall under the general title of *Foundations of Modern Biology*. Textbooks written for school and university use are generally too long and too technical for adult use, and in any case the latest developments may not be discussed, even though these may be of great interest to an adult class. However, one modern text in physics which should be attractive to the serious adult student of physics is "The Mainstream of Physics" by A. Beiser (Addison-Wesley, 1962). The value of this book for private study is enhanced by the production of a study guide as a companion volume.[16]

Periodicals such as *Discovery, Scientific American, The New Scientist, Endeavour, Science Progress,* and *The Advancement of Science* all contain articles of interest to adult classes, while the book review sections give useful information on current publication in various scientific fields. Special mention may perhaps be made of the section "New Books for the General Reader" published by courtesy of the National Book League in *The Advancement of Science.* Students should, of course, be encouraged to use local library services and guidance from the tutor as to the sort of books to look for should be given. The local library may, on occasion, be prepared to mount an exhibition of books recommended by the tutor for a particular class.

The demand in some subjects for vocational and specialist courses has already been mentioned in certain cases. This is a trend which seems likely to continue. Moreover, as science teaching at the school level increases and scientific knowledge among the general public becomes more widespread, one can expect the demand for adult classes in science to continue to grow. One factor which certainly favours this situation is the use of television as an additional visual aid. The sciences are excellent material for direct television teaching. Complex processes can be demonstrated in such a way as to give every viewer a front row view, and short snatches of film can be introduced at the appropriate moment. Unfortunately, there can be no discussion and so the television lecture, however good it may be of itself, should stimulate interest in the adult class where questions and discussion can complete the educational process. Co-operation between the bodies providing adult classes in science and the television companies should lead to further demand for tutor-led discussion classes.

It is pointless to argue about the proportion of adult teaching which should be devoted to science subjects. What is important is to ensure that the science which *is* taught is of the best quality. The demand for science classes is growing and will continue to grow. At every stage of development it must cater for the educational needs of the adult.

NOTES TO CHAPTER IX

[1] See, for example, D. S. L. CALDWELL, *The Organisation of Science in England: A Retrospect* (Heinemann, 1957) and T. KELLY, *A History of Adult Education in Great Britain* (University of Liverpool Press, 1962). For references to developments in particular localities, see the *Select Bibliographies of Adult Education* published by the National Institute of Adult Education, 1952, and 1962.

[2] There have been many articles on the place and value of science in adult education. The following are among the more important:

Science and Adult Education, Report of the Sixth Conference of the British Institute of Adult Education (1927).

Natural Science in Adult Education, Paper No. 8 of the Adult Education Committee of the Board of Education (H.M.S.O., 1927).

Science Teaching in Adult Education, *Ann. Rept. Brit. Assoc. for the Advance. of Sci.* (1933), p. 330.

Science in Adult Education, *ibid* (1937), p. 305.

Science in Adult Education, *Advance. of Sci.*, **VI**, 131 (1949).

The Teaching of Science in Adult Education, Oxford University Delegacy for Extra-Mural Studies (1951).

R. PEERS, *Science in the Extra-Mural Work of Universities* (Universities Council for Adult Education, 1954).

T. J. PICKVANCE, The Sciences in the Extra-Mural Work of Universities, *Adult Educ.*, **XXVII** (1954), p. 205.

Aspects of Adult Education, W.E.A. Working Party Report (1960).

Science in Extra-Mural Studies, University of Bristol Department of Extra-Mural Studies Annual Report, 1960–61.

D. VANSTONE, A Proper Balance, *Adult Educ.*, **XXIV** (1961), p. 67.

Adult Educ., **XXXV** (May, 1962) was mainly devoted to science teaching in adult education and contains several useful articles.

[3] For a fuller discussion see *Tutors' Bull.*, 2nd Series, No. 4 (May, 1932), p. 1.

[4] Though it does not deal specifically with the teaching of science, some useful ideas on the general techniques of teaching adult groups are to be found in M. F. CLEUGH, *Educating Older People* (Tavistock Publications, 1962).

[5] For a general discussion of some methods of teaching science in adult classes see H. D. TURNER, Developments in Science Teaching, *Adult Educ.* **XXVII** (1954), p. 35.

[6] See T. L. MACDONALD, Astronomy for Adult Classes, *J. Adult Educ.*, **V**, (1931), p. 317.

Idem, Some Experiments in Science, *Tutors' Bull.*, 2nd Series, No. 19 (Feb., 1937), p. 14.

[7] Some thoughts on the content of such a course have been given by R. D. HARRISON, *Adult Educ.*, **XXXV** (1962), p. 19.

[8] See C. COCHRANE, Physics and the Adult Class, *J. Adult Educ.*, **V** (1931), p. 186.

Idem A Tutorial Class in Physics, *ibid.*, **VI** (1933), p. 146.

The Teaching of Science in Adult Education, Oxford University Delegacy for Extra-Mural Studies (1951).

R. D. HARRISON, Science for the Layman, *Bulletin of the Institute of Physics and The Physical Society* (Feb., 1963), p. 34.

[9] E. MATSUKAWA and P. C. RUSSELL, Adult Education and Nuclear Physics *Adult Educ.*, **XXX** (1957), p. 59.

Idem, Modern Physics as an Extra-Mural Course, *Adult Educ.*, **XXX** (1958), p. 143.

[10] Cf. H. H. SWINNERTON, Geology for Adult Students, *Tutors' Bull.*, 2nd Series, No. 4 (May, 1932), p. 17.

[11] For a general discussion of the place of the museum in adult education see H. A. MIERS, Museums and Art Galleries in Adult Education, *J. Adult Educ.*, **VI** (1934), p. 399.

Museums and Adult Education, National Institute of Adult Education (1956).

S. THOMPSON, The Museum and Art Gallery in Adult Education, *Scot. Adult Educ.*, **18** (1956), p. 23.

E. M. HUTCHINSON, Museums and Adult Education—an Idyll, *Adult Educ.*, **XXIX** (1956), p. 33.

[12] The general problems of the teaching of biology were considered at the Oxford University Delegacy for Extra-Mural Studies Conference on *The Teaching of Science in Adult Education* (published 1951).

G. F. LEE, Teaching about Living Things, *Further Educ.*, **III** (1949–50), p. 236.

R. W. CROSSLAND, The Teacher of Biology in Adult Education, *Adult Educ.*, **XXIX** (1956), p. 45.

F. W. R. BRAMBELL, The Educational Value of Zoology, *Univ. Quart.*, **VIII** (1953–54), p. 62.

F. H. WHITEHEAD, A Suggestion for Botanical Work in Adult Education Classes, *Rewley House Papers*, **III**, IV (1955–56), p. 24.

L. BENTLEY and L. P. TURNBULL, They Find Out for Themselves, *Adult Educ.*, **XXXV** (1962), p. 14.

For a consideration of the place of field work see R. S. R. FITTER, Field Studies and Further Education, *Adult Educ.*, **XXXI** (1958), p. 203.

[13] Cf. G. PATTISON, Anthropology for Adults, *Tutors' Bull.* (Spring, 1953), p. 10.

[14] See, for example, pp. 44–46 of *Natural Science in Adult Education*, Paper No. 8 of the Adult Education Committee of the Board of Education (H.M.S.O., 1927).

P. J. KING, Science as a Subject for Adult Study, *Tutors' Bull.*, 1st Series, No. 26 (Dec., 1928), p. 19.

V. DAVIS, A Plea for the Further Study of Science and Scientific Methods in Adult Classes, *Tutors' Bull.*, 2nd Series (July, 1931), p. 22.

And, for a modern plea, H. J. FYRTH and M. GOLDSMITH, Science in History—an Experiment, *Adult Educ.*, **XXXV** (1963), p. 360.

[15] See R. W. CROSSLAND, The Reading of Adult Students attending Science Courses: an Investigation of Reading Difficulties, *Adult Educ.*, **XXV** (1952), p. 205.

[16] Some views on suitable books for classes in the physical sciences will be found in an article by R. D. HARRISON [*Adult Educ.*, **XXXV** (1962), p. 37].

CHAPTER X

PSYCHOLOGY

Philip A. D. Gardner

A DEPENDABLE feature of all organised systems of education is that as the learner progresses he is given increasing opportunity to make choices. Initially others decide what will be taught, how it will be taught and even when it will be taught. Subsequently, the learner is expected to express his own particular interests and abilities and eventually to select and study, from those available subjects of his own choosing. Sometimes the choice made represents rather lack of particular interests or abilities; sometimes it is determined by the demands of vocational necessity.

For most people it is only when formal academic and vocational education is completed that real freedom of choice is attained and something like educational self-realisation becomes possible. At this point the existence of a system of adult education is critical. Those responsible for its organisation recognise this unique opportunity and attempt to meet it by providing the widest possible range of subjects for study. Indeed, so varied are the subjects offered in a typical compendium of adult classes in a large centre that choice becomes something of a problem.

THE CHOICE OF PSYCHOLOGY

Psychology, as it happens, has always been one of the more popular choices. Some general reasons for this are obvious enough. In the first place though interest in and speculation about human behaviour is as old as man himself, many people continue to regard psychology as a relatively new and modern subject. No doubt some adult students are attracted to the subject because they think of it in this way. For such it is a fashionable choice.

The opportunity to study psychology formally is restricted to adults. Many other subjects offered in adult courses have been studied at earlier stages in school. The new element with these is a difference in approach or treatment, notably in critical systematisation or evaluation. But with psychology it is the subject itself that is being encountered for the first time in an educational setting.

Perhaps the subject is popular chiefly because we live in an age increasingly aware of the practical uses (and abuses) of psychology and much impregnated with psychological ideas. Psychological assessments of one kind or another are likely to be made of oneself or one's children in school or college or work, perhaps even at the point of entry. Important personal and social outcomes may depend upon the result. Much emotion if nothing else is aroused. Psychological techniques are said to be employed in advertising and these carry their assault right into the home on television. More and more people we know fall ill in ways which are said to involve psychological factors. And apart from these immediate personal encounters psychological viewpoints are continually presented in press, radio and television. Articles and programmes about the relationships between parent and child, about delinquency, marital problems and mental health have become difficult to avoid. This means that before students come to adult classes they often have some personal experience of events that were given a psychological import, or that they already have some notions about the nature of psychology. This immediate interest is valuable, but it often expresses itself in prejudiced viewpoints and restricted ideas about the subject.

In these and many other ways psychology has become important in everyday affairs. Beyond these practical affairs too the tendency is increasingly to see life in the large in psychological terms. The success, the overall satisfaction of a life, perhaps even its meaning, tend more and more to be viewed in a psychological context rather than in an ethical or religious setting. The artist as he reports and comments on the human scene has in our time done so with an extra dimension—the psychological. If the arts are not rendered easier thereby, they are nonetheless more telling when understood. Proper appreciation demands a psychological accompaniment.

And if this is true of the arts it is also so in the practical, objective, fact-finding world of science. Only the immediate excitement of atomic research and its awful practical potential has led us mistakenly to describe the age as a nuclear one. There never was an age so focussed on man and his ways, so thoroughly prepared to examine and re-examine him in an objective scientific way, and so properly described as psychological. In such circumstances a general interest in psychology is inevitable.

STUDENT SELF-SELECTION

In consequence it might be expected that all adult students at some time would dip into psychology at least once. This it seems does happen and all adult psychology classes have a proportion of members whose interest is general and who merely want to be informed. When this is achieved they pass on to some other subject. It is equally clear, however, that many students do not chance upon psychology as one more, albeit important roundabout in the fairground of knowledge but rather have come to the fair only because the particular study is available. In other words, a high degree of self-selection among students is probably the rule in psychology classes. Interest is personal and precise rather than general and diffuse.

This individual and personal attractiveness of psychology has at least three sources. First, there are students who choose the subject because in their work they deal chiefly with people and they seek to increase their professional effectiveness. Strictly practical applications are envisaged on joining and they come to learn the rules. Among such students are teachers and nurses, salesmen and journalists, almoners and personnel managers and the like. Often such students have had some previous instruction in psychology during their training, but they judge that it has been insufficient or not of the right sort, or that they need a refresher. Often it seems they wish to repeat the original learning under the freer conditions of the typical adult class where they can interrupt, call for clarification, argue and criticise; activities unlikely to have been allowed, far less tolerated or encouraged, in their professional courses. Some undoubtedly come because in the interval following the original training course they have had many puzzling experiences with clients and have had time to rethink and assimilate theory and practice and to mature as people: they look for a new synthesis.

Such students are often a distinct asset in a class. They contribute authentic material for discussion and views and criticisms that advance the arguments constructively. At the same time they can be something of a liability in that they often find it hard to see that psychology neither developed out of their own specialised interest nor has it tailor-made answers for their particular use. Occasionally, too, some of these students give indications that it is not psychology they are interested in but getting control over others. For them psychology offers principally techniques by which they can more surely get their own way: that the real aim is a fuller understanding of situations in which individuals attempt to exercise control over others hardly interests them.

Secondly, some students choose psychology not to improve professional proficiency and control over others but to increase their understanding of the behaviour of others with whom they work and live. Occasionally this motive stems from real problems or anxieties connected with the behaviour of others with whom they associate. Relatives or friends of individuals who have had a mental illness, parents of children whose marriages are unhappy or look like breaking up or even the partner whose spouse needs special understanding are cases in point. So too are parents of puzzling adolescents or problem children, though these usually feel some responsibility for the disturbing behaviour and wish eventually to pass beyond merely understanding to some sort of active interference with the situation. Most such students have no familiarity with psychology and simply believe it will help in a situation where much else has failed them.

These students are mostly women and mostly parents. Psychology, it has often been suggested, makes more appeal to women. It is certainly the case that the proportion of women in psychology classes is high. (This, however, is probably to be found in other subjects also.) Perhaps women, because they have closer relationships with more people than have men, encounter more human relations problems. As mothers of families they are certainly at the vortex of many relationships and perhaps are compelled to take greater responsibility for the smooth conduct of relationships. Part of this rôle involves them as mediators between opponents and absorbers of the emotional tensions of others.

If human relationships are more important in the life of women, psychology will in turn interest and attract them in greater numbers.

Lastly, not a small proportion select psychology because they want to know about their own personality and behaviour. Occasionally this is no more than egocentred curiosity but often it stems from personal unhappiness, from feelings of inadequacy or anxiety or failure or even from neurotic disturbance. Many such students sit through a session without disclosure, but as a class proceeds some seek assistance and openly admit why they came in the first place. The writer's first adult class provided a good example of this. At the conclusion of the fourth meeting a youngish middle-aged woman, whom the writer had not noticed before, approached him saying she suffered from overwhelming headaches. These occurred about once a week. When she had an attack she was unable to go to work. She had seen her doctor about it on several occasions and had taken all he prescribed without any alleviation of the symptoms. After hearing what had been said at the class meetings she was convinced the symptoms were psychogenic and should be treated as such. It was suggested she should return to her doctor and ask him to refer her to the outpatient psychiatric department of a local hospital. She was very willing to do this but the following week reported that her doctor thought this was a lot of nonsense and would not refer her. She was very distressed. It was then suggested that she simply attend the outpatient department without being referred. The tutor himself was then ill and did not return to the class for some ten weeks. On resuming he at once noticed a strikingly brunette student wearing a vividly-patterned green mantilla-like head scarf. He could not recall ever having seen her before and assumed she must have joined the class in his absence. At the conclusion of the meeting, however, she came to report that she was the student who had had the headaches, that she had attended the outpatient clinic as suggested and was completely recovered. She then disclosed that she had come to the class in the first place because of the headaches hoping to get relief somewhere. She certainly bore little resemblance to her former self. Such advantageous use of a psychology class is, however, rather exceptional ! More often the problem is partly divulged and no ready solution is at hand.

Such individuals are often a continuing burden to the tutor and to the other students, particularly to those others with similar motives for attending. It is often difficult to know what to do for such students or how to handle them. If they seek help the situation is eased but usually they do not do so openly nor would they be able to accept or act upon suggestions made, if they did. Not all tutors would agree with Harding[1] that to ignore this aspect of a course in psychology is to "waste an opportunity and neglect a danger", nor would all tutors feel competent to assume responsibility for this area of student learning. But that in psychology classes this is a real problem that ought to be taken seriously none will deny. It is false to think that psychology is "a merely intellectual discipline without repercussions on the whole personality of the student".[2]

Without conscious distresses or overt difficulties some students undoubtedly choose psychology because they imagine it has something special to offer. They expect some sort of magic that goes beyond the commonplace, that will make life richer, fill a want, be a completion for them. Usually such students are quickly discouraged and disappointed by the subject, but others go on hopefully, seemingly finding something of what they sought.

Thus in choosing psychology, the student is likely to express more than a general desire for knowledge or even for this particular knowledge. His motives are likely to be very complex and mixed and to include some he would not be able to report if asked. But relatively few attempts have been made even to find out what students say about why they chose a particular subject.[3]

PSYCHOLOGY COURSES

With this recognition of student motives it might be expected that the tutor in psychology would approach his subject in a way strikingly different from that of tutors in other subjects, that he would attempt to meet the student needs at least in some measure. Generally this is not so. The usual syllabus topics for adult psychology classes reflect a straight academic approach that for the most part ignores the student's personal motives. Introductory courses list topics such as are found (and probably were) in any academic textbook. Industrial psychology courses often seem to suggest they will proceed as if work was an academic interest only. Experimental psychology courses seem often concerned to remain laboratory tied.

It may well be that this detachment from and ignoring of the known situation is a necessary condition of operation, at least initially. But all psychology tutors know well enough that the more their offered course touches off real motives the larger will be the number who are attracted to the class. Hence the partial recognition of actual needs in course titles like "Psychology and Everyday Life" or "The Psychology of Personal Relationships" or "About Ourselves": "Personality in the Making" or "Mental Health". Even with titles of this sort, however, the treatment is likely to be detached and impersonal. The personal relationships and mental health spoken about are those of hypothetical other people. Unless the class demands that it shall be otherwise, the tutor has little choice. It is always fascinating, however, to notice how closely and with what interest case histories are attended to even when they are pure inventions. Presumably this is the justification behind the case discussion method of teaching human relations in industry.

Usually, tutors offer courses in which the material is broken down into those areas or specialities currently accepted as theoretically distinguishable or practically useful in teaching, or in which they themselves are interested or knowledgeable. This happens even in introductory courses where aspects of behaviour like motivation or learning, developmental or social psychology tend to be taken one at a time and discussed separately. In so doing, the tutor merely reflects the contemporary psychological scene with its unities and divisions. Provided some attempt is made to relate the particular areas dealt with to the whole subject, and this in turn to the whole of behaviour including non-psychological approaches, this would seem unobjectionable. Often, however, it seems students may get too restricted, too partial and particular a viewpoint from a single class and then believe this to be the whole.

Common divisions of the subject made are as follows:

       Child and Developmental Psychology
       Educational Psychology
       Experimental Psychology
       Social Psychology
       The Psychology of Personality
       Clinical and Abnormal Psychology
       Industrial Psychology.

University undergraduates who read psychology are likely to be taught the subject broken down in this fashion. Some tutors follow this plan in adult classes sometimes making even more restricted divisions of the subject such as "The Psychology of Religion", "Psychoanalysis and Our Time", "Stages of Human Development" and "Psychological Tests and Assessments".[4] Clearly such classes cater better for students who already have some general knowledge of psychology. But more frequently, perhaps in adult studies, tutors offer (at least in titles) wider divisions of the subject in which several of the recognised areas overlap. Titles like 'Man in the Making", "Human Relations", "Psychologists at Work", "Mental Health", "Psychology and Everyday Affairs" and "Psychology Films"[5] suggest a coverage which is very comprehensive. The chances are that some conflict of aim arises where the tutor wants to limit himself to an area of the subject which he has delineated and the class want to know everything about the subject and everywhere it applies.

In introductory courses this width of view seems proper and the right approach is to tell the students "about" psychology. Perhaps the chief gain to the tutor comes from the challenge that this presents. Not only does it call for wide knowledge and versatility to do this in exposition, but for much courage and humility to keep *en rapport* with the class thereafter when question and discussion takes over. The point is that introductory courses are more difficult to conduct in some ways. In the Scottish Universities this is recognised in the time-honoured tradition that the professor in a department should take the "Ordinary" class.

This raises sharply the issue of what we hope to achieve in psychology classes with adults and how far we are prepared to meet the students in satisfying their demands.

DISCUSSION IN CLASS

The discussion period allows and is intended to allow the student to express his opinions, ask his questions and contribute to the processes that shape the class. In psychology classes this opportunity clearly opens more doors for the expression of personal motives than in most other classes. It seems likely that in proportion as discussion can be exploited for permissive personal expression the more the group will judge the class successful. But individual needs clash and discussion may merely encourage individual rivalry and aggression. It is often apparent that a student is trying to get the tutor to take his view and wants psychological ideas to be aligned with his own. Often he wants to persuade the other members of the class to follow his own line.

This individual struggle in group discussion to get what you came for, using ordinary language in what seems like logical discourse, has therefore to be recognised by the tutor as a therapeutic opportunity in which attitudes may be expressed, emotion given outlet and relief and support obtained. To put the matter differently, discussions all proceed at more than one level with more than one meaning, and in discussion of psychology this presents an opportunity through which understanding can be increased if the experience can be assimilated. Whether this occurs or not depends on the relationships within the class and between class and tutor, on the size of the class, the balance of views in the group and the unusualness or challenge of the particular viewpoint. Clearly, abnormal points of view and argument present the greatest challenge and most serious problem for the class and tutor but even these can be expressed and contained under some conditions.

AIMS

No tutor would regard therapeutic outcomes as the major aim of adult psychology classes. Classes are not primarily therapeutic groups. Nor would the tutor imagine he was trying to turn out psychologists, though some class members may like this idea. Initially, the aim would seem to be to inform about the subject, describing what psychologists aim at, how they proceed and what they think are the probable conclusions. This allows the student to stand outside the subject and observe and comment without being involved. The tutor can encourage this by talking of psychology and psychologists from a non-professional position explaining the history or rationale of a point of view or theory, without identifying himself with it. This comes naturally to an uncommitted eclectic and amounts to description, exposition or explanation.

For many students who wish to know about the subject or how it impinges in a general way on their work, this approach is probably sufficient. There are several accounts of this factual approach to teaching various branches of the subject[6], though in a different setting from this present one.

But as Raven wisely points out in another connection "in Psychology there is more to be learnt than can be taught".[7] To know about psychology is not the end. Clearly a further aim is to make the student aware that psychology is not so much a body of fact about which you can get to know, as a mode of approach or way of thinking about human behaviour. And even students who have no desire or intention to make use of psychology professionally should be able to appreciate something of what it means to look and interpret from the psychological position. A knowledge of psychology that resulted in no change in attitude to the behaviour of others would be a partial acquisition only. It may not be possible to agree entirely with Raven (who after all is talking about clinical psychologists) in this matter, but clearly an aim in adult classes is to achieve this end in some part. He suggests that the student should become "aware of the difficulties in the way of understanding other people", "tolerant of other people's opinions and loyalties", "aware that his own training and interests determine what he attends to, what he ignores and how he interprets what he notices, aware of the variability of the information" with which he works. In short, he should become aware of the complexity of the process by which we collect, organise and use our observations of the behaviour of others and, in consequence, a little less emotionally attached to our own personal thinking and judgement of others. If this aim is often not achieved with adult students it must be admitted that professional psychologists by no means universally attain it either.

Perhaps the last aim of psychology worth noting is one concerned with the student's own perception of himself and attitude to himself. This is even less likely to be achieved. As a result of courses in psychology it might well be expected that the student would attempt some review of himself. The earliest evidence of such happening is often shown by students who begin to discuss their own upbringing and family setting and try to see how this might have affected them as individuals. It is a short intellectual step to go further and ask "What kind of person am I?" but the answer is hard to find and perhaps even more difficult to accept. While taking psychology courses a small number of students, not all disturbed or neurotic, usually begin to enquire in this sort of way and some are prepared to pursue the matter as far as they can, seeking psychotherapeutic support or accepting psychoanalytic insights as they do so. But without going so far some self-awareness would be a worthwhile aim. Insights into oneself of any kind or at any level may result in more realistic personal adjustments, in better relationships with others with whom one lives or works, in improved mental health and more enjoyment of living. Wolfle[8] identifies these three objectives as (1) acquainting the student with "the most important and most generally accepted facts, principles and hypotheses", (2) developing "the habit of critical and objective analysis of psychological problems of modern society" and (3) enabling the student "to understand his own personal problems and to achieve personally and socially desirable solutions of those problems".

Harding,[9] accepting these aims, goes further in suggesting that psychology is an important element in the education of our times. He points out that the position of the subject, combining something of the outlook of the arts and of science, makes its contribution rather special. On the one hand its interests extend into literature, history and ethics, into subtle and complex aspects of human behaviour, and on the other its ideal is a full application of scientific method. This disciplined study of important areas of human behaviour Harding regards as leading to refined insights and extended understanding. Something of the values and viewpoints of both arts and science subjects are shared by psychology. If, as Harding maintains, "the educational processes that can occur in studying psychology and only in studying it intensively" are central for our time, we are fortunate in that few problems of motivation in this area of learning arise other than those of our own making.

That psychology has an important, perhaps vital, rôle to play in education and particularly in adult education seems to be more and more realised. There is a sense in which as physics and chemistry are basic to the natural sciences, psychology is basic to man and society.

THE WHOLESOME OUTCOME

When a tutor or teacher professes an academic discipline and engages in teaching it year in year out, it must be supposed that he finds the subject interesting (or once did) and thinks it is of some importance or value. If in addition he shows enthusiasm for the subject, comparing its contribution with that of others to the advantage of his own, defending it from attack and regarding it as of central importance, this is likely to affect his teaching and effectiveness. Apart from method of presentation, interest, value and enthusiasm for a subject are attributes of the tutor which are of great importance in determining his impact.

In this respect psychology tutors are like others and attempt to teach their subject as ably as they can and to emphasise its importance in human affairs. To a point this is fact and is accepted by the class but beyond a certain point too much enthusiasm seems to the writer to be undesirable in adult education. It is clear that too narrow and too naïve an enthusiasm for his subject leads at least the more mature adult students to regard the tutor as out of contact with reality or a pure academic—to the detriment of his teaching. And in psychology something like this danger always lurks. Not a few tutors in psychology are likely to give the impression that the fundamental questions are most completely answered in psychological terms. They may really believe this themselves and they may even be right, but as tutors of adult students this narrow allegiance is unfortunate. Mature students will properly recoil from this all comprehending claim and thereafter entertain an undue scepticism about psychology and psychologists. This is, however, a healthier response than following the tutor and coming to believe not only that there is a psychological explanation for everything but that the psychological one is the most important. The chief danger is perhaps not allegiance to the subject as a whole but to some part of it or some school of thought. The dedicated, psycho-analytically oriented tutor is such a person. His effect is often to divide a class into disciples and opponents. It seems that too great and too narrow an allegiance on the part of the tutor to his own subject or any part of it is particularly inappropriate with adult students.

One difference between adult students and others is that the adult has a great fund of actual knowledge and experience (beyond that of the tutor in certain fields). This, though seldom well digested or systematised, results in his being less ready to accept what the tutor says uncritically. The adult student is less gullible, less satisfied with one answer and perhaps, in the best sense, more doubtful and sceptical about what he sees and hears. The really mature student may even doubt whether formal educational experiences lead to more understanding and wholeness.

It seems well to recognise, therefore, that in teaching psychology the tutor should avoid giving any impression of omnipotence about the subject and should try to place it in perspective in relation to other human knowledge. If in some senses it may be thought central in others it is not. Its centrality stems from its panoramic overview of other human activities rather than from a denial of their authenticity and value.

In particular it seems unfortunate if students of psychology get the idea that life can be lived at the level of a continuous psychological exposition or commentary or that this is how psychologists live. It is important to bring home to students that the viewpoint of the psychologist is a highly unusual one, justified only for specific ends and tolerable only if reintegrated into the complex of ordinary living.

The psychologist questions ordinary common-sense notions about people. He sees human behaviour as far more complicated than ordinary people do. He finds behaviour more difficult to understand and explain. If this leads to uncertainty and confusion and immobilises the student, as it may well do, the tutor has failed to put the human picture together again. He must make it clear that this complicated approach is usually made for a short time in a specific setting. Thus the many views about the delinquent other than that he is simply bad are not entertained merely to confuse issues. Some of these views may in fact clarify our thinking about delinquents and result in more adequate action. The special viewpoint of psychology has *somehow* to be taken account of when we live out our ordinary lives.

The psychologist, too, in surveying objectively the field of human behaviour, stands back emotionally from his material. This cuts him off temporarily from others and renders him emotionally unresponsive. The student may learn to do this but he has also to learn to re-engage emotionally with others after this psychological cut-out. The whole justification of the exercise is lost if normal relationships cannot be restored perhaps on a new level of insight.

The psychologist as he observes human behaviour becomes a spectator, who no longer interferes with others. This means that he ceases to have aims for them, to be concerned about them or to feel responsible towards them. This irresponsibility must after a time be given up and more usual "interfering" behaviour reappear. The lack of aim can be justified only if it leads to clearer understanding of aims as found in society.

Lastly, the psychologist, in looking at human behaviour, describes and explains but does not judge. This suspension of values is an unusual and perhaps dangerous background to action. Ordinary living demands the reintroduction of value judgements. If there is enhanced understanding of current values the exercise may be justified.

Thus psychology as a discipline results in acting and thinking in unusual and even peculiar ways. It results in restricted and specialised viewpoints and explanations which do not easily fit back into ordinary living. Students attending courses in psychology may readily adopt some of these unusual positions and ideas in relation to other persons and fill the rôle of "amateur psychologist". This is an undesirable outcome.

An adequate exposition of the subject must attempt to reconcile all this with ordinary everyday living and experience, and perhaps in the long run accept that the psychological viewpoint is one more, a relatively new one, perhaps an all-important one, certainly a challenging one that has to be integrated by the student for himself into his own life and times.

NOTES TO CHAPTER X

[1] Education through Psychology, *Bull. Brit. Psychol. Soc.*, **28**, p. 5.

[2] *loc. cit.*

[3] W. E. FLOOD and R. W. CROSSLAND, The origins of interest and motives for study of Natural Sciences and Psychology among adult students in voluntary courses, *Brit. J. Edal. Psychol.*, **XVIII**, pp. 105–117.

D. E. G. BLOWMAN, How some university entrants see Psychology, *Bull. Brit. Psychol. Soc.*, **32**, p. 34.

[4] Titles of courses in the *Adult Studies: Programme of Classes in the City of Glasgow*, 1961–62.

[5] Titles of courses offered in the *Programmes of Classes in the City of Glasgow* over the years 1957–63.

[6] (a) Report of the Committee on undergraduate training in *Psychol. Quart. Bull.*, **9**, p. 337.

(b) The teaching of Social Psychology, *Bull. Brit. Psychol. Soc.*, **33**, p. 15,

(c) Teaching of Experimental Psychology, *Bull. Brit. Psychol. Soc.*, **37**, p. 1,

(d) The Teaching of Personality Development—edited by PAUL HALMOS, *Sociol. Rev.*, Monographs 1 and 2. The University of North Staffordshire. Keele.

[7] The selection, work and promotion of clinical psychologists, *Bull. Brit Psychol. Soc.*, **19**, p. 9.

[8] The first course in Psychology, *Psychol. Bull.*, November, 1942.

[9] Education through Psychology, *Bull. Brit. Psychol. Soc.*, **28**, p. 5.

SELECT BIBLIOGRAPHY

GENERAL

THOMAS KELLY, *A Select Bibliography of Adult Education* (National Institute of Adult Education, London, 1952).

C. D. LEGGE and R. D. WALLER, *First Handlist of Studies in Adult Education* (National Institute of Adult Education, 1952).

C. D. LEGGE and R. D. WALLER, *Second Handlist of Studies in Adult Education* (National Institute of Adult Education, 1953).

C. D. LEGGE, *Guide to Studies in Adult Education, 1953* (National Institute of Adult Education, 1954).

C. D. LEGGE, *Guide to Studies in Adult Education, 1954* (National Institute of Adult Education, 1955).

C. D. LEGGE, *Guide to Studies in Adult Education, 1955* (National Institute of Adult Education, 1956).

C. D. LEGGE, *Guide to Studies in Adult Education, 1956* (National Institute of Adult Education, 1957).

C. D. LEGGE, *Guide to Studies in Adult Education, 1957* (National Institute of Adult Education, 1958).

C. D. LEGGE, *Guide to Studies in Adult Education, 1958* (National Institute of Adult Education, 1959).

THOMAS KELLY, *A Select Bibliography of Adult Education in Great Britain* (National Institute of Adult Education, London, 1962).

J. W. HUDSON, *The History of Adult Education*, (1851).

R. PEERS, *Adult Education: a Comparative Study*, (Routledge & Kegan Paul, 1958).

J. F. C. HARRISON, *Learning and Living, 1790–1960*, (Routledge & Kegan Paul, 1961).

THOMAS KELLY, *A History of Adult Education in Great Britain* (Liverpool University Press, 1962).

N. DEES, Adult Education in Western Germany, *Highway*, *44* (March, 1953), pp. 208–11.

PERIODICALS

Tutors' Bull., Nos. 1–105, 1922–56 (Association of Tutors in Adult Education).

Adult Educ., Half-yearly, **I-VI**, 1926–34 (British Institute of Adult Education).

Adult Educ., Quarterly, **VII-XXXIII**, 1934–60; Bi-monthly, **XXXIV, . . .** (1960 . . .) (in progress) (British Institute of Adult Education till 1949, then N.I.A.E.).

Rewley House Papers, Annually (publication irregular, 1944–54), **I-II** (1927–49); **III** . . . (1949 . . .) (in progress) (Oxford University Extra-Mural Delegacy).

Scot. Adult Educ., Thrice yearly, No. 1 . . . (1951 . . .) (in progress) (Scottish Institute of Adult Education).

HISTORY

E. A. LYLE, History: the Key Subject in Adult Education, *Adult Educ.*, **XVI** (1943-4), pp. 7-15.

N. M. HOLLEY, History for the Adult Student, *Adult Educ.*, **XX** (1947-8), pp. 87-94.

Ministry of Education, *Teaching History* (H.M.S.O., 1952).

N. DEES, History in Adult Education, *J. Inst. Educ. Durham Univ.*, **3**, No. 17 (May, 1952), pp. 21-2.

N. DEES, The History Class, *Highway*, *43* (April, 1952), pp. 251-4.

ECONOMICS

G. D. H. COLE, The Teaching of Economic History and Theory, *J. Adult Educ.* **I** (1926-7), pp. 227-35.

A. JOHNSON, *Some Problems Associated with the Teaching of Economics*, (Central Joint Advisory Committee on Tutorial Classes, 1950).

Economics Association, *The Teaching of Economics* (1961).

INTERNATIONAL RELATIONS

G. W. KEETON, International Relations in Adult Classes, *Adult Educ.*, **VII** (1934-5), pp. 25-33.

J. F. C. HARRISON, Towards an Interpretation of International Relations, *Adult Educ*, **XXI** (1948-9), pp. 75-81.

International Relations: Some Study Material, *Adult Educ*, **XXIV** (1951-2), pp. 82-5.

E. MONKHOUSE, The Teaching of International Relations, *Tutors' Bull.*, No. 95/96 (June-September, 1954), pp. 12-15.

C. O. HOULE and C. A. NELSON, *The University, the Citizen and World Affairs* (American Council on Education, Washington, 1956).

S. H. BAILEY, *International Studies in Great Britain*, Chapter II (Oxford University Press, 1933).

MODERN LANGUAGES

E. V. GATENBY, Language Learning for Adults, *Adult Educ.*, **XIX**, No. 2 (December, 1946), pp. 105-14.

C. L. M. HARDING, The Students' View, *Adult Educ.*, **XXXIV**, No. 5 (January, 1962), p. 258.

P. H. HARGREAVES, Modern Language Classes, *Adult Educ.*, **XXXIV**, No. 1 (May, 1961), pp. 23-7.

J. HARVARD, *Teaching Adults to Speak a Foreign Language* (University of London Press, 1961).

W. C. R. HICKS, Language Learning for Adults, *Adult Educ.*, **XVI**, No. 4 (June, 1944), pp. 172-84.

Incorporated Association of Assistant Masters, *The Teaching of Modern Languages* (1949), p. 359.

L. KOCHLAN, Why to Learn and How to Teach a Foreign Language, *Adult Educ.*, **XXII**, No. 1 (September, 1949).

Ministry of Education, Pamphlet No. 29, *Modern Languages*, (H.M.S.O., 1956, p. 119).

P. NEWMARK, An Approach to Modern Language Teaching, *Adult Educ.*, **XXIII**, No. 1 (June, 1950), pp. 44–55.

P. NEWMARK, Conflict in Teaching Methods, *Adult Educ.*, **XXXIV**, No. 5 (January, 1962), p. 238.

M. A. L. SCULTHORP, The Language Laboratory, *Adult Educ.*, **XXXIV**, No. 5 (January, 1962), p. 249.

E. M. STACK, *The Language Laboratory and Modern Language Teaching* (Oxford University Press, 1960).

P. NEWMARK, E. LOCKWOOD and R. RUDDOCK, Three Studies in Problems of Language, *Adult Educ.*, **XXIV**, No. 3 (Winter, 1951), pp. 193–206.

ENGLISH LANGUAGE AND LITERATURE

H. E. POOLE, *The Teaching of Literature in the W.E.A.*, (Brit. Inst. Adult. Educ., **1938**).

D. S. BLAND, Literature and Adult Education, *Cambridge J.*, **IV** (1950), pp. 172–80.

R. HOGGART, English Studies in Extra-Mural Education, *Univ. Quart.*, **5**, No. 3 (May, 1951), pp. 251–7.

T. W. THOMAS, Practical Criticism and the Literature Class, *Adult Educ.*, **XXIV**, 1 (Summer, 1951), pp. 20–9.

D. HEWITT, The Literary Critic and the Historian, *Tutors' Bull.*, No. 88 (October, 1952), pp. 10–14.

R. HOGGART, Poetry and the Adult Group, *Adult Educ.*, **XXV** (Winter, 1952), pp. 180–8.

J. L. STYAN, Practical Literature, *Tutors' Bull.*, No. 92 (Autumn, 1953), pp. 15–18.

R. WILLIAMS, Text and Context, *Tutors' Bull.*, No. 93/94 (December, 1953–March, 1954), pp. 19–22.

P. A. W. COLLINS, Research Groups in English Literature, *Tutors' Bull.*, Nos. 100–2 (September, 1955–March, 1956), pp. 20–1.

D. BUTTS, The Development of Literature Teaching in the Oxford Tutorial Classes, *Rewley House Papers*, **III** (1958–9), pp. 13–19.

R. HOGGART, *Teaching Literature*, National Institute of Adult Education in co-operation with Department of Adult Education (University of Hull, 1963).

J. L. STYAN, *Elements of Drama*, (Cambridge University Press, 1960).

ART

W. G. CONSTABLE, Art and Adult Education, *Adult Educ.*, **VII** (1934–5), pp. 8–17.

T. BODKIN, *Adult Education in the Fine Arts*, (Selly Oak Colleges, Birmingham, 1937), p. 16.

F. W. JESSUP, The Arts and Adult Education, *Adult Educ.*, **XXI** (1948-9), pp. 117-27.

MUSIC

K. T. ELSDON, Music Appreciation: An Experiment, *Adult Educ.*, **XXX** (1957-8), pp. 127-34.

H. HAVERGAL, Music as a Form of Adult Education, *Scot. Adult Educ.*, No. 18 (December, 1956), pp. 14-18.

G. BUSH, *Musical Creation and the Listener*, (Muller, London, 1954).

R. L. JACOBS, Linking Musical Appreciation with Harmony, *The Music Teacher* (March, 1951).

E. PYBUS, *The Teaching of Musical Appreciation* (C.J.A.C., 1953) p. 28.

P. T. BARFORD, The Place of Formal Analysis in Adult Musical Education, *Monthly Musical Record*, **VIII** (1951), pp. 120-5.

R. L. JACOBS, The Aims of Musical Appreciation, *Tutors' Bull.*, No. 84 (October, 1951), pp. 17-9.

P. M. WALTERS, Music and the Adult Student, *Adult Educ.*, **V** (1930-2), pp. 423-9.

J. H. HIGGINSON, Music and the Man in the Street, *Adult Educ.*, **XI**, No. 1 (September, 1938), pp. 54-63.

G. THOMAS, Music in Wales, *Adult Educ.*, **XI** (1938-9), pp. 199-212.

W. H. MELLERS, Musical Culture Today, *Tempo*, No. 7 (June, 1944), pp. 2-5.

W. H. MELLERS, New Audiences for Old, *Tempo*, No. 12 (September, 1945), pp. 5-8.

The W.E.A. and Musical Appreciation, Hinrichsen's Musical Year Book, 1945-6, pp. 240-2.

H. W. SHAW (ed.), *Musical Education*, (Hinrichsen, 1946) p. 259.

N. TOWNSHEND, A W.E.A. Music Club, *Highway*, **XL** (September, 1949), pp. 236-8.

PSYCHOLOGY

O. L. ZANGWILL, Doubts and Queries about Psychology, *Rewley House Papers*, **III**, 2 (Summer, 1953), pp. 38-43.

Workers' Educational Association, Association of Tutors in Adult Education, and Central Joint Advisory Committee for Tutorial Classes, *Psychology and the Adult Student* (1937).

J. HEMMING, Humanity is Various, *Highway*, **XL** (1948-9), pp. 184-**6.**

R. RUDDOCK, The Psychology of Psychologists, *Highway*, **XLIII** (1951-2), pp. 135-7.

APPENDIX

The extra-mural area of the University of Glasgow consists of the City of Glasgow and the counties of Argyll, Ayrshire, Bute, Dumfriesshire, Dunbartonshire, Kirkcudbright, Lanarkshire, Renfrewshire, Stirlingshire and Wigtownshire. Classes are arranged by the University Extra-Mural Committee in conjunction with the Education Committees of the Local Authorities. In the years 1961–62 and 1962–63 (see *Annual Report University of Glasgow Extra-Mural Education Committee*, 1962–63) the figures for standard classes were:

A. CLASS PROGRAMME

TABLE I—AREA DISTRIBUTION OF CLASSES

	Classes		Enrolments	
	1961–62	1962–63	1961–62	1962–63
Argyll	13	13	285	238
Ayrshire	23	28	428	641
Bute	4	5	57	140
Dumfriesshire	35	37	719	678
Dunbartonshire	9	9	154	152
Glasgow	100	115	2423	2994
Kirkcudbright	6	6	112	96
Lanarkshire	32	40	497	667
Renfrewshire	10	18	146	260
Stirlingshire	11	19	253	254
Wigtownshire	7	9	111	231
Totals	250	299	5185	6351

TABLE II—TYPES OF CLASSES

	1961–62	1962–63
Tutorial Classes	7	6
Sessional Classes	157	178
Courses of 13–19 meetings	26	22
Courses of 10–12 meetings	35	46
Courses of 3–9 meetings	25	47
Totals	250	299

Table III—Subject Distribution of Classes

	Number of Classes	
	1961–62	1962–63
Archaeology	12	9
History	18	23
Geography	9	6
International and Commonwealth Affairs	12	10
Social Studies	35	62
Law	6	5
Philosophy	9	9
Psychology	15	8
Religion	7	8
Physical Sciences	13	19
Biological Sciences	23	35
Other Scientific Studies	14	7
English Language and Literature	17	20*
Ancient Language and Literature	9	4
Modern Languages, Literature and Culture	18	22
†Celtic Languages	—	4†
Music	15	22
Visual Arts	18	26
Totals	250	299

*Figures for 1962–63 include 1 class in Scottish Literature.
†This category was not included in 1961–62 (1962–63, 1 class in Welsh, 3 classes in Gaelic).

Table IV—Occupation of Students

Occupation	1961–62 %	1962–63 %
Housewives	20·9	25·2
Manual Workers	4·9	5·1
Non-manual, technical and supervisory workers	29·4	39·6
Teachers	16·7	15·5
Professional workers	16·9	10·4
Not in paid work	8·9	4·2
Unknown	2·3	—
Totals	100	100

B. For a variety of additional extension and residential work the figures were:

UNIVERSITY EXTENSION LECTURES

"The British-Soviet Pamirs Expedition, 1962"	170
Poetry Recital	130
Film and discussion—"President Kennedy's T.V. Conference"	76

WEEKEND SCHOOLS

"Britain and the Common Market" (in co-operation with the National Dock Labour Board), Aberfoyle	35
"Productivity" (in co-operation with the National Dock Labour Board), Ayr	30
Study of Soviet Education (in co-operation with Department of Soviet Institutions), University	58
Natural History (for Wigtownshire students), Teesdale	9

ONE-DAY SCHOOLS AND CONFERENCES

"Broadcasting and Society", Ayr	51
"Costume in the Theatre", Dumfries	9
"Professional Production in the Theatre", Dumfries	24
"Agriculture and the Common Market" (in co-operation with N.F.U.), Castle Douglas	37
"Britain and Europe" (in co-operation with South-West Scotland Federation of Townswomen's Guilds), University	150
"The Scottish Economy", Ayr	14
"Mime and Movement" (in co-operation with Guild of Players), Dumfries	20
"The Winter's Programme in Glasgow Theatres", University	55
"Drama", Dumfries	20

SUMMER SCHOOL

Dublin	35

OTHER COURSES

"Youth" (residential course in co-operation with S.W.R.I.), Largs	35
Residential Adult Education Course for Women (in co-operation with Glasgow Corporation Further Education Department), Largs	25
Course of six lectures at Penninghame Open Prison, Newton Stewart	45

University Week—"Scotland's Natural Heritage"	64
Two-day course for Glasgow senior school pupils—Introduction to university studies	333
Course for Austrian Trade Unionists, Newbattle Abbey	40

COURSES FOR STUDENTS OF FURTHER EDUCATION COLLEGES (IN CO-OPERATION WITH GLASGOW CORPORATION)

Logan and Johnson Pre-Nursing College, at University and Newbattle Abbey	66
Langside College, at Dalston Hall by Carlisle	40

TUTORS' CONFERENCES AND COURSES; OPENING OF SESSION MEETINGS

"The Tutor and the Class", Ayr	10
"Recent Trends in Adult Education", Castle Douglas	20
"After Pilkington", Newton Stewart	35
"After Pilkington", Dumfries	80
Residential Conference on language teaching (in conjunction with West of Scotland Joint Committee), Aberfoyle	28
Training course for tutors in Music, University	15

Type of Course	Attendance
University Extension Courses	376
Summer School	35
Week-end and One-day Schools and Conferences	512
Other Courses	542
Courses for Students of Further Education Colleges	106
Tutors' Conferences and Courses; opening of session meetings	188
Total	1759

Classes are also arranged for the West of Scotland Joint Committee on Adult Education (in the City of Glasgow and the counties of Dunbartonshire, Lanarkshire, Renfrewshire, and Stirlingshire). These classes are in the main language and public speaking classes in the City of Glasgow. Of these in the year 1962–63 there were 84 with an enrolment of 2,605 students. The total provision in this type of class with these five Authorities was 114 classes with a total enrolment of 3,124 students.

In the total extra-mural area of the University of Glasgow under these arrangements in 1962–63 adult student enrolments were therefore: University extra-mural classes 6,351; University extension and residential courses and conferences 1,759; in co-operation with the West of Scotland Joint Committee 3,124; total 11,234 (approximately 2 per cent of the adult population of the area).

STUDENTS' BACKGROUND

In the year 1961-62 a survey of students within the City of Glasgow showed the proportion of men to women as roughly 2 : 3: that the largest single age-group of students is between 21 and 30 years (25·3 per cent): that the highest occupational category is that of professional people (28·6 per cent): and that the number of manual and distributive workers is 5 per cent. In educational background, 32 per cent of the students had received full-time formal continuing education to the age of 20 and 35 per cent possessed a university degree or its professional equivalent.

CATEGORIES AND EXPERIENCE OF TUTORS EMPLOYED

Members of the staff of the university compose just less than 50 per cent of the total number of tutors employed. Of the tutors not employed by the university 44·4 per cent were teachers, 29·4 per cent members of other professions; 11·1 per cent married women with professional or academic qualifications; and 8 per cent ministers of religion.

There were 19 per cent of tutors taking a class for the first time; 53 per cent d taken classes for one or two previous sessions; and 28 per cent for ᴠ ᴠ n two previous years.

DULT EDUCATION GROWTH

A comparison of class figures for the year 1962–63 with those for 1958 ᴠ9 ᴠ thin the City of Glasgow shows that the number of completed successful courses for the year 1962–63 represents an overall increase of 35 per cent in the five-year period or a mean annual increase of 7 per cent. This can be compared with the national figures published by the U.C.A.E., which show 1ᴠ per cent more classes in the year 1961–62 than in the year 1958–59, a mean annual increase of less than 3 per cent. Over the same five-year period the tᴄ ᴠl enrolment figure in Glasgow indicates a more effective provision in that t. umber of students rose by 45 per cent against a 35 per cent increase in cla ᴠes—more than a *pro rata* expansion. In terms of averages the number of students per class rose from 23 to 26.